THE Sugarless Cookbook

COOKING WITH THE NATURAL SWEETNESS OF FRUIT

by Nellie G. Hum

FRONT COVER

Fresh Strawberry Pie, page 9

The Sugarless Cookbook
by Nellie G. Hum

Second Printing — August, 1988

Hum Publishing
395 Second Avenue
Ottawa, Ontario
K1S 2J3

Canadian Cataloguing in Publication Data
Hum, Nellie G.
The sugarless cookbook

Includes index.
ISBN 0-919845-52-5

1. Sugar-free diet — Recipes. 2. Cookery (Fruit).
I. Title.

RM237.85.H85 1987 641.5'63 C87-098041-6

Photography by
Patricia Holdsworth
Patricia Holdsworth Photography
Regina, Saskatchewan

Designed, Printed and Produced in Canada by
Centax of Canada
Publishing Consultant and Food Stylist: Margo Embury
Designer: Blair Fraser
1048 Fleury Street
Regina, Saskatchewan, Canada S4N 4W8
(306) 359-3737 Toll-Free 1-800-667-5844

TABLE OF CONTENTS

Introduction 4

Pies and Tarts 5

Cakes and Cake Desserts 18

Frostings and Toppings 30

Cookies, Bars, Squares and Turnovers 36

Desserts: Baked, Fruit and Cold 45

Fillings 58

Puddings 62

Pancakes and Crêpes 69

Sweet Sauces and Syrups 76

Muffins, Quick Breads, Popovers and Scones 83

Butters, Jams and Spreads 93

Treats 100

Beverages 102

Index 107

Helpful Tips (See Index Listing) 108

INTRODUCTION

We all use fruit juices for drinking but I also use them for baking. For years I have experimented making cookies, pies, cakes, etc. using no sugar, no artificial sweeteners and no salt. The results have inspired me to create 250 recipes sweetened with fruit and fruit juices instead of sugar, honey, molasses, corn syrup, cyclamates or aspartames. My preference for fruit and fruit juices to the traditional sugar or any other sweetener, has the added advantage of increasing vitamins and minerals in any diet.

For weight watchers, skim milk powder has been used instead of whipping cream in the Lemon Chiffon Pie, Pineapple Cheesecake, Low-Calorie Fruit Bavarian, etc. For the cholesterol-conscious cook, vegetable oil has been used in Muffins, Pancakes, Quick Breads and many other recipes. For sodium-restricted diets, the absence of salt has not deterred the fine taste in any of the finished products.

My collection of recipes requires ingredients commonly available in every kitchen. I hope that you will enjoy this nutritious way of sweetening as much as I.

ADJUSTING RECIPES:

Whole-Wheat Flour — 1 cup (250 mL) of finely ground whole-wheat flour may be substituted for 1 cup (250 mL) of all-purpose flour. Stir lightly, do not sift whole-wheat flour before measuring.

For 1 cup (250 mL) butter, margarine or shortening, use ¾ cup (175 mL) **oil.**

For 1 tbsp. (15 mL) butter, margarine or shortening, use 2¼ tsp. (11 mL) **oil.**

CANNED FRUIT AND FRUIT JUICES:

Read labels for sugar content when buying canned goods. **Unsweetened** fruit packed in its own juice, or in any other juice, should be used whenever canned fruit is required in these recipes.

Unsweetened fruit juices and **unsweetened** concentrated fruit juices have been used in recipes throughout this book. If unsweetened concentrated **pineapple** juice is unavailable, substitute unsweetened concentrated **apple** juice.

Pies and Tarts

TWO-CRUST 9" (23 cm) PIE PASTRY

Sift together:

2¼ cups	**(550 mL)**	**sifted all-purpose flour**
***½ tsp.**	**(2 mL)**	**baking powder (optional)**

Cut in coarsely with pastry blender until size of small peas:

¾ cup	**(175 mL)**	**shortening**

Sprinkle over mixture, while tossing with a fork:

5 tbsp.	**(75 mL)**	**ice water**

Press dough firmly into 2 balls. Roll each on lightly floured board, from centre outwards, to ⅛" (3 mm) thickness. Fold 1 in half; fit loosely into pie plate.

Spoon in filling. Trim off overhanging edge of pastry. Moisten edge with milk. Cover filling with remaining pastry which has been slashed in several places to allow steam to escape. Press bottom and top edges to seal.

For a plain crust, trim off excess pastry. For a fluted crust, trim off ½" (1.3 cm) beyond plate. Roll pastry edge under and on rim of plate. Flute edge by using thumb and index finger of one hand on the outside and index finger of other hand on the inside edge of pastry.

Brush with milk. Bake according to recipe chosen.

* Makes a lighter and a more tender crust.

TO CHECK ACCURACY OF OVEN TEMPERATURE:

Place an oven thermometer in the oven when baking. This will verify the oven temperature.

TWO-CRUST 9" (23 cm) PIE PASTRY

(using oil)

Sift together:

2¼ cups	**(550 mL)**	**sifted all-purpose flour**
***½ tsp.**	**(2 mL)**	**baking powder (optional)**

Mix in lightly with a fork:

½ cup	**(125 mL)**	**PLUS 1 tbsp. (15 mL) corn oil**

Sprinkle over mixture; mix well:

4 tbsp.	**(60 mL)**	**ice water**

Press dough firmly into 2 balls. Place each between 2 sheets of plastic wrap. Roll, from centre outwards, to ⅛" (3 mm) thickness. Remove top sheet; turn over onto pie plate; remove other sheet. Fit pastry loosely into plate.

Spoon in filling. Complete as for Two-Crust Pie Pastry, page 5.

* Makes a lighter and a more tender crust.

ONE - CRUST 9" (23 cm) PIE PASTRY

Sift together:

1¼ cups	**(300 mL)**	**sifted all-purpose flour**
***¼ tsp.**	**(1 mL)**	**baking powder (optional)**

Cut in coarsely with pastry blender until size of small peas:

½ cup	**(125 mL)**	**shortening**

Sprinkle while tossing mixture with a fork:

3 tbsp.	**(45 mL)**	**ice water**

Press dough firmly into a ball. Roll on lightly floured board, from centre outwards, to ⅛" (3 mm) thickness. Fold in half; fit loosely into pie plate.

For a plain crust, trim off excess pastry. For a fluted crust, see Two-Crust Pie Pastry, page 5. See photograph front cover.

* Makes a lighter and a more tender crust.

ONE-CRUST 9" (23 cm) PIE PASTRY

(using oil)

Sift together:

1⅓ cups	**(325 mL)**	**sifted all-purpose flour**
***¼ tsp.**	**(1 mL)**	**baking powder (optional)**

Mix in lightly with a fork:

⅓ cup	**(75 mL)**	**corn oil**

Sprinkle over mixture; mix well:

2 tbsp.	**(30 mL)**	**ice water**

Press dough firmly into a ball. Place it between 2 sheets of plastic wrap. Roll, from centre outwards, to ⅛" (3 mm) thickness. Remove top sheet; turn over onto pie plate; remove other sheet. Fit pastry loosely into plate.

For plain crust, trim off excess pastry. For fluted crust, see Two-Crust Pie Pastry, page 5.

*Makes a lighter and a more tender crust.

BAKED PIE SHELL

Prepare One-Crust Pie Pastry (above), or page 6. Prick pastry all over with fork after trimming or fluting. Bake at 450°F (230°C) until brown, 15 to 18 minutes.

FOR BEST RESULTS IN MAKING PIES:

Have all ingredients as cold as possible.

CHEESE PASTRY

Sift together:

1 cup	**(250 mL)**	**sifted all-purpose flour**
¼ tsp.	**(1 mL)**	**baking powder**

Cut in coarsely with pastry blender until size of small peas:

⅓ cup	**(75 mL)**	**shortening**

Mix in:

⅓ cup	**(75 mL)**	**grated sharp cheese**

Sprinkle:

3 tbsp.	**(45 mL)**	**ice water**

Toss with fork just until flour is moistened. Press dough firmly into a ball. Roll out on lightly floured board to fit a 9" (23 cm) pie plate. Fold in half; fit it loosely into pie plate. Spoon in filling. Bake according to recipe chosen.

CRUMB PIE CRUST

Mix well:

***1 cup**	**(250 mL)**	**fine crumbs**
½ tsp.	**(2 mL)**	**cinnamon (optional)**
5 tbsp.	**(75 mL)**	**softened butter OR margarine**

Press mixture firmly on bottom and sides of a 9" (23 cm) pie plate. Chill ½ hour before filling or bake at 350°F (180°C) for 10 minutes. Cool before filling.

*Make fine crumbs using graham or soda crackers, zwieback, toasted dry bread, dry cake or cookies.

TO MAKE FINE CRUMBS:

Use a blender or a food grinder OR put crackers, etc. in a plastic bag, crush into crumbs with rolling pin, then pass through a sieve.

SELF-CRUSTING COCONUT PIE

Sift together:

½ cup	**(125 mL)**	**sifted all-purpose flour**
1½ tsp.	**(7 mL)**	**baking powder**

Beat together:

4	**(4)**	**eggs, well beaten**
3 tbsp.	**(45 mL)**	**vegetable oil**
¾ cup	**(175 mL)**	**milk**
¾ cup	**(175 mL)**	**toasted shredded coconut**

Beat flour mixture into egg mixture.

Add and beat until blended:

¾ cup	**(175 mL)**	**unsweetened pineapple juice**
½ cup	**(125 mL)**	**unsweetened concentrated fruit juice**

Pour into a 10" (25 cm) pie pan. Bake at 350°F (180°C) until firm, 30 to 40 minutes.

Serves 6-8.

FRESH STRAWBERRY PIE

Prepare Baked Pie Shell, page 7.

Wash, pat dry and hull:

1 qt.	**(1 L)**	**fresh strawberries**

Reserve 1 cup (250 mL) strawberries, set remainder stem end down in pie shell.

Combine in a saucepan until smooth:

2 tbsp.	**(30 mL)**	**cornstarch**
4 tbsp.	**(60 mL)**	**unsweetened concentrated pineapple OR apple juice, defrosted**

Add, stir and cook until thickened, cool slightly:

¾ cup	**(175 mL)**	**unsweetened red grape juice**
1 cup	**(250 mL)**	**reserved strawberries, crushed**

Pour over berries. Chill until set, about 2 hours.

Using pastry tube, pipe around edge of pie with:

Whipped Cream, page 30

Serves 6. See photograph on front cover.

LEMON CHIFFON PIE

Prepare Crumb Pie Crust, page 8.

Warm over low heat until dissolved:

1 tbsp.	**(15 mL)**	**gelatine**
1/3 cup	**(75 mL)**	**unsweetened concentrated pineapple OR apple juice, defrosted**

Stir in; chill until thick but not set:

4 tbsp.	**(60 mL)**	**lemon juice**
1 1/2 cups	**(375 mL)**	**unsweetened pineapple juice**
		grated rind of 1 lemon

Add; beat until volume doubles:

1/2 cup	**(125 mL)**	**instant skim milk powder OR**
3 tbsp.	**(45 mL)**	**noninstant skim milk powder**

Pour into pie shell. Chill until set. Spread top with:

Mock Whipped Cream, page 30

Serves 6.

CRANBERRY-APPLE PIE

Prepare Baked Pie Shell, page 7.

Cook until skins of cranberries pop; stir occasionally:

1 3/4 cups	**(425 mL)**	**cranberries, picked over and washed**
4	**(4)**	**medium apples, peeled and finely sliced**
3/4 cup	**(175 mL)**	**unsweetened concentrated apple juice, defrosted**
4 tbsp.	**(60 mL)**	**water**

Combine; add hot mixture; stir and cook until thick:

2 tbsp.	**(30 mL)**	**cornstarch**
3 tbsp.	**(45 mL)**	**water**

Pour into pie shell. When cooled, using pastry tube, pipe around edge of pie with:

Whipped Cream, page 30.

PUMPKIN PIE

Prepare One-Crust Pie Pastry, page 6 or 7. Chill.

Combine in a mixing bowl until smooth:

3 tbsp.	**(45 mL)**	**unsweetened concentrated apple juice, defrosted**
2 tsp.	**(10 mL)**	**cornstarch**

Add and beat until blended:

1 cup	**(250 mL)**	**canned pumpkin**
¾ cup	**(175 mL)**	**pureéd, cooked sweet potato**
2	**(2)**	**eggs**
5 tbsp.	**(75 mL)**	**unsweetened concentrated pineapple juice, defrosted**
3 tbsp.	**(45 mL)**	**unsweetened concentrated apple juice**
1½ tsp.	**(7 mL)**	**cinnamon**
½ tsp.	**(2 mL)**	**nutmeg**
½ tsp.	**(2 mL)**	**ginger**

Stir in:

½ cup	**(125 mL)**	**milk**

Pour into pie shell. Bake 10 minutes at 450°F (230°C) reduce to 350°F (180°C) until firm in centre, 35 to 45 minutes. Cool. Garnish with:

Whipped Cream, page 30

Serves 6.

CUSTARD PIE

Prepare One-Crust Pie Pastry, page 6 or 7. Chill.

Beat just until blended:

4	**(4)**	**eggs, slightly beaten**
1¾ cups	**(425 mL)**	**milk**
½ tsp.	**(2 mL)**	**vanilla**

Mix in:

½ cup	**(125 mL)**	**unsweetened concentrated mixed (apple and pineapple) juice, defrosted**

Pour into pie shell. Bake 10 minutes at 450°F (230°C), lower to 325°F (160°C) for 30 to 40 minutes. Cool. Garnish with:

Whipped Cream, page 30

Serves 6.

PINEAPPLE SPONGE PIE

Prepare One-Crust Pie Pastry, page 6 or 7. Chill.

Cream until soft and creamy:

2 tbsp.	**(30 mL)**	**butter OR margarine, room temp.**
2 tbsp.	**(30 mL)**	**instant skim milk powder OR**
2 tsp.	**(10 mL)**	**noninstant skim milk powder**

Beat in:

2	**(2)**	**egg yolks**
2 tbsp.	**(30 mL)**	**flour**

Add; mix well:

1¼ cups	**(300 mL)**	**undrained crushed pineapple**
6 tbsp.	**(90 mL)**	**unsweetened concentrated pineapple juice**

Beat until stiff, then fold in pineapple mixture:

2	**(2)**	**egg whites**

Pour into pie shell. Bake 10 minutes at 425°F (220°C), lower to 325°F (160°C), for 30 to 40 minutes. Cool. Garnish with:

Whipped Cream, page 30

Serves 6.

CREAM PIE

Pour warm:

Cream Filling, page 58

Into:

Baked Pie Shell, page 7

Top with:

Meringue, page 34 OR
Whipped Cream, page 30

Chill before spreading whipped cream.

Serves 6.

VARIATIONS:

BANANA CREAM PIE: Pour ¼ of Cream Filling into pie shell, top with sliced bananas. Add remaining Cream Filling and proceed as above.

COCONUT CREAM PIE: Add ¾ cup (175 mL) toasted, shredded coconut to Cream Filling. Proceed as for Cream Pie and sprinkle the Whipped Cream with more toasted coconut.

FRESH BLUEBERRY PIE

Prepare Two-Crust Pie Pastry, page 5 or 6.

Combine in a large bowl until smooth:

2 tbsp. (30 mL) cornstarch
1 tsp. (5 mL) lemon juice
5 tbsp. (75 mL) unsweetened concentrated pineapple juice, defrosted

Mix in:

4 cups (1 L) fresh blueberries, washed, drained

Line pie plate with half the pastry. Fill with blueberry mixture. Trim off overhanging edge of pastry. Roll remaining dough for upper crust or cover lattice fashion with ½" (1.3 cm) strips of pastry. Starting at centre, lay strips, leaving ½" (1.3 cm) between strips. Repeat crosswise, but weave strips over and under original ones.

Flute edge by using thumb and index finger of 1 hand on the outside and index finger of other hand on inside edge of pastry. Brush top with milk. Bake 10 minutes at 450°F (230°C), reduce to 350°F (180°C) for 30 minutes or until a golden brown.

Serves 6.

FRESH PEACH PIE

Prepare Two-Crust Pie Pastry, page 5 or 6.

Combine in a large bowl until smooth:

2 tbsp. (30 mL) cornstarch
½ tsp. (2 mL) almond extract
4 tbsp. (60 mL) unsweetened concentrated pineapple juice, defrosted

Mix in:

4 cups (1 L) peeled, sliced peaches

Line pie plate with half the pastry. Fill with peach mixture. Complete as for Fresh Blueberry Pie, above.

Serves 6.

APPLE PIE

Prepare Cheese Pastry, page 8.

Combine in large bowl until smooth:

2 tsp.	**(10 mL)**	**cornstarch**
½ tsp.	**(2 mL)**	**cinnamon**
½ cup	**(125 mL)**	**unsweetened concentrated apple juice, defrosted**

Mix in:

6	**(6)**	**medium apples, peeled, thinly sliced**

Pour into pastry.

Sift together:

½ cup	**(125 mL)**	**all-purpose flour**
2 tsp.	**(10 mL)**	**noninstant skim milk powder OR**
2 tbsp.	**(30 mL)**	**instant skim milk powder**
		pinch of white pepper

Cut in with pastry blender until crumbly:

2 tbsp.	**(30 mL)**	**cold butter OR margarine**

Mix in, then sprinkle over apple mixture:

2 tbsp.	**(30 mL)**	**grated cheese**

Bake 10 minutes at 400°F (200°C), lower to 350°F (180°C) until brown, about 45 minutes.

Serves 6.

RAISIN PIE

Prepare Two-Crust Pie Pastry, page 5 or 6.

Line a 9" (23 cm) pie plate with half of pastry.

Fill with:

Raisin Filling, page 61

Trim off overhanging edge of pastry. Roll remaining dough for top. Cut slits in centre to allow steam to escape. Moisten edge of bottom crust with milk. Place top pastry over filling. Press top and bottom edges to seal. Trim off excess pastry. Brush with milk. Bake 10 minutes at 425°F (220°C), lower to 325°F (160°C) until golden brown, 25 to 30 minutes.

Serves 6.

TART SHELLS

In the:

Two-Crust Pie Pastry, page 5 or 6

Replace the ice water with:

unsweetened fruit juice

Divide dough into 14 parts. Roll each part ⅛" (3 mm) thick; cut with 4" (10 cm) round cutter. Fit into tart or muffin pans.

Makes 14, 3" (7.6 cm) shells.

VARIATIONS:

UNBAKED TART SHELLS: Fill tart shells ½ to ⅔ full of your favourite filling. Bake according to recipe chosen.

BAKED TART SHELLS: Prick pastry all over with fork. Bake at 425°F (220°C) until golden brown, 15-18 minutes.

KIWI CREAM TARTS

Fill Baked Tart Shells, above, ⅔ full with:

Cream Filling, page 58

When ready to serve, place on each tart:

2 (2) slices of kiwi, peeled

Makes 12. See photograph page 16A.

BANANA CREAM TARTS

Fill Baked Tart Shells, above, ⅔ full with:

banana slices
Cream Filling, page 58

Garnish with:

Whipped Cream, page 30

Makes 12.

LEMON TARTS

Fill Baked Tart Shells, page 15, ⅔ full with:

Lemon Chiffon Pie Filling, page 10

Chill until firm. Garnish with:

Whipped Cream, page 30

Makes 12.

PINEAPPLE TARTS

Prepare Baked Tart Shells, page 15

Beat in a saucepan until blended:

1	**(1)**	**egg**
1 tbsp.	**(15 mL)**	**cornstarch**
2 tbsp.	**(30 mL)**	**unsweetened concentrated pineapple juice, defrosted**
6 tbsp.	**(90 mL)**	**juice drained from crushed pineapple**

Cook and stir until thick. Mix in:

19 oz.	**(540 mL)**	**crushed pineapple, well-drained**
½ tsp.	**(2 mL)**	**almond extract**

Spoon into tarts shells. When cold, garnish with:

Whipped Cream, page 30

Makes 12.

FRESH FRUIT TARTS

Fill Baked Tart Shells, page 15, ¾ full with:

blueberries, strawberries, sliced peaches OR pears

Cook and stir until thick:

1 tbsp.	**(15 mL)**	**cornstarch**
¾ cup	**(175 mL)**	**unsweetened apple OR pineapple juice**
2 tbsp.	**(30 mL)**	**unsweetened concentrated apple OR pineapple juice**

Spoon a tablespoon (15 mL) of glaze over filled tarts. Chill. Garnish with:

Whipped Cream, page 30

Makes 12.

Fresh Fruits in Jelly, page 52
Kiwi Cream Tarts, page 15

APPLE MERINGUE TARTS

Prepare Unbaked Tart Shells, page 15.

Beat until blended:

1¾ cups	**(425 mL)**	**applesauce**
2	**(2)**	**egg yolks**
½ tsp.	**(2 mL)**	**cinnamon**
4 tbsp.	**(60 mL)**	**unsweetened concentrated apple juice, defrosted**

Spoon into tart shells. Bake 10 minutes at 450°F (230°C), lower to 325°F (160°C). While tarts are baking, prepare:

Meringue, page 34

Pile meringue on tarts. Bake 15 to 20 minutes.

Makes 12.

TO KEEP OVEN CLEAN:

Place a cookie sheet under pies when baking. It will protect against pies bubbling over.

TO FOLD EGG WHITES:

Add mixture to stiffly beaten egg whites. Fold by moving a wooden spoon, a rubber or plastic scraper, up, over and down until blended.

FOR BEST RESULTS IN BEATING EGG WHITES:

Allow egg whites to reach room temperature before beating to achieve highest volume.

Beat egg whites in a glass or stainless steel (not plastic) bowl. Avoid using an aluminum bowl as it will darken egg whites.

TO PREVENT MERINGUE FROM SHRINKING WHILE BAKING:

Spread meringue on pies or cakes until it touches the pastry edges or baking dishes, respectively.

TO TEST FRESHNESS OF AN EGG IN SHELL:

Place the egg in a cup almost filled with water. If it floats, it is rotten. If it sinks and lies on its side, it is fresh. If it sinks and stands erect, it is still edible.

Cakes and Cake Desserts

PLAIN CAKE

Sift together:

1⅓ cups	**(325 mL)**	**sifted all-purpose flour**
1½ tsp.	**(7 mL)**	**baking powder**
¼ tsp.	**(1 mL)**	**baking soda**

Cream until soft and creamy:

4 tbsp.	**(60 mL)**	**butter OR margarine, room temp.**
2 tsp.	**(10 mL)**	**noninstant skim milk powder OR**
2 tbsp.	**(30 mL)**	**instant skim milk powder**

Beat in:

1	**(1)**	**egg, beaten**

Add flour mixture alternately with:

⅔ cup	**(150 mL)**	**unsweetened concentrated mixed fruit juice, defrosted**

in 2 lots, beating only until blended. Pour into an oiled 8" (20 cm) square or round nonstick cake pan. Bake at 350°F (180°C) until brown, 35 to 40 minutes. Leave cake in pan on wire rack 10 minutes. Remove from pan. Serve with any sweet sauce or spread with:

Buttery Icing, page 34

Serves 6-8.

TO STORE CONCENTRATED FRUIT JUICE:

Store concentrated fruit juice in freezer, after covering opened can with foil, or pour into a jar with a plastic cover. When juice is needed, dip a spoon or a knife in very hot water and dig out the amount required.

SPONGE CAKE

Sift together 4 times:

¾ cup	**(175 mL)**	**sifted cake flour**
2 tbsp.	**(30 mL)**	**cornstarch**
1½ tsp.	**(7 mL)**	**baking powder**
¼ tsp.	**(1 mL)**	**baking soda**

Beat until soft peaks form:

4	**(4)**	**large egg whites**

Add and beat until stiff and glossy:

⅛ tsp.	**(0.5 mL)**	**cream of tartar**

Beat until very thick:

4	**(4)**	**large egg yolks**

Gradually beat into yolks:

5 tbsp.	**(75 mL)**	**unsweetened concentrated fruit juice, defrosted**

Beat in flour mixture 3 tbsp. (45 mL) at a time.

Fold into egg whites. Pour into an ungreased wax-paper-lined 9" (23 cm) tube or square pan. Bake at 325°F (160°C) for 40 to 50 minutes. Invert on wire rack for 1 hour.

Serves 6.

BOSTON CREAM PIE

Make a Sponge Cake but bake it in an ungreased wax-paper-lined 8" (20 cm) round cake pan. Cool. Cut to make 2 layers.

Spread between layers:

Cream Filling, page 58 OR
Custard Cream Filling, page 59

Cover top and sides with one of:

Whipped Cream, page 30
Low-Calorie Whipped Cream, page 31
Low-Calorie Whipped Topping, page 31
Mock Whipped Cream, page 30

Serves 6-8.

FRUIT FLAN

Fruit Flan is easy to make and delightful to serve.

Sift together:

7/8 cup	**(205 mL)**	**sifted all-purpose flour**
1½ tsp.	**(7 mL)**	**baking powder**
¼ tsp.	**(1 mL)**	**baking soda**

Cream until soft and creamy:

2 tbsp.	**(30 mL)**	**butter OR margarine, room temp.**
2 tsp.	**(10 mL)**	**noninstant skim milk powder OR**
2 tbsp.	**(30 mL)**	**instant skim milk powder**

Beat in thoroughly:

1	**(1)**	**egg**

Add flour mixture alternately with:

½ cup	**(125 mL)**	**unsweetened concentrated mixed fruit juice, defrosted**

in 2 lots, beating only until blended. Pour into a lightly oiled 10" (25 cm) nonstick flan pan. Bake at 350°F (180°C) until brown, 18-20 minutes. Cool 5 minutes in pan. Unmould. The depression becomes the top side of cake. Cool.

Prepare glaze by combining:

4½ tbsp.	**(67 mL)**	**cornstarch**
¾ cup	**(175 mL)**	**unsweetened concentrated apple OR pineapple juice, defrosted**

Add, cook and stir until thick; cool:

2 cups	**(500 mL)**	**water**

Reserve ¾ cup (175 mL) glaze and spread remainder to cover depression, topping it with an arrangement, in circular pattern, of:

strawberries, peeled, sliced peaches, peeled, sliced kiwi , mandarin orange segments, canned sliced peaches OR apricots (drain and pat dry) OR blueberries

Spoon remaining glaze to cover fruit. Garnish with:

Whipped Cream, page 30

Serves 8.

CUSTARD FRUIT FLAN

Prepare Fruit Flan, page 20 but fill the depression with:

Custard Filling, page 59

Arrange in a circular pattern on top of custard:

strawberries, peeled, sliced peaches, peeled, sliced kiwi, mandarin orange segments, canned sliced peaches OR apricots (drain and pat dry) OR blueberries

Prepare glaze to coat fruit by combining:

5 tsp.	**(25 mL)**	**cornstarch**
5 tbsp.	**(75 mL)**	**unsweetened concentrated apple OR pineapple juice, defrosted**

Add, cook and stir until thick; cool:

¾ cup	**(175 mL)**	**water**

Spoon to cover fruit. Garnish with:

Whipped Cream, page 30

Serves 8. See photograph page 32A.

BANANA CAKE

Sift together:

2 cups	**(500 mL)**	**sifted all-purpose flour**
2 tsp.	**(10 mL)**	**baking powder**
¾ tsp.	**(4 mL)**	**baking soda**

Cream until soft and creamy:

2 tsp.	**(10 mL)**	**noninstant skim milk powder OR**
2 tbsp.	**(30 mL)**	**instant skim milk powder**
½ cup	**(125 mL)**	**butter OR margarine, room temp.**

Beat in:

1	**(1)**	**large egg, well beaten**
1½ cups	**(375 mL)**	**mashed ripe banana (3 large)**
3 tbsp.	**(45 mL)**	**unsweetened concentrated pineapple juice**
3 tbsp.	**(45 mL)**	**water**

Stir in flour mixture. Pour into an oiled 8" (20 cm) square or round nonstick pan. Bake 40 to 50 minutes at 350°F (180°C). Spread with:

Broiled Banana Meringue, page 35

Serves 8-10.

FRESH FRUIT CAKE

Sift together:

1¾ cups	**(425 mL)**	**sifted all-purpose flour**
2 tsp.	**(10 mL)**	**baking powder**
½ tsp.	**(2 mL)**	**baking soda**

Combine in a bowl:

6 tbsp.	**(90 mL)**	**unsweetened concentrated orange juice, defrosted**
1 tbsp.	**(15 mL)**	**lemon juice**
1	**(1)**	**peach, peeled, cut in small pieces**
1	**(1)**	**medium apple, peeled, grated**
		grated rind of 1 orange

Cream until soft and creamy:

5 tbsp.	**(75 mL)**	**butter OR margarine, room temp.**
2 tbsp.	**(30 mL)**	**instant skim milk powder OR**
2 tsp.	**(10 mL)**	**noninstant skim milk powder**

Beat in:

1	**(1)**	**large egg, well beaten**
1	**(1)**	**small ripe banana, mashed with fork**

Add fruit mixture. Stir in dry ingredients. Pour into a buttered wax-paper-lined 11" X 7" (28 X 18 cm) pan. Bake 40 to 50 minutes at 350°F (180°C) or until toothpick inserted in centre comes out clean.

Serves 9-11.

TO KEEP CUT FRESH FRUIT FROM DISCOLOURING:

Sprinkle fruit with lemon or pineapple juice immediately after cutting.

TO PREVENT FRUIT SINKING TO BOTTOM OF BATTER:

Dust raisins, dates, etc. with a little flour, to keep them suspended in batter.

FOR MORE EVEN BAKING OF CAKES, ETC.:

Turn pan front to back after baking 12 to 15 minutes.

DRIED FRUIT FRUITCAKE

Finely chop fruit; soak 4 hours or overnight:

3	**(3)**	**figs, stems removed**
5	**(5)**	**pitted prunes**
5	**(5)**	**apricots**
6	**(6)**	**pitted dates**
¼ cup	**(50 mL)**	**raisins**
½ cup	**(125 mL)**	**unsweetened orange juice**
2 tsp.	**(10 mL)**	**grated orange rind**

Cook and stir until mixture is just moist, about 8 minutes. Cool.

Sift together:

1¼ cups	**(300 mL)**	**sifted all-purpose flour**
1½ tsp.	**(7 mL)**	**baking powder**
½ tsp.	**(2 mL)**	**baking soda**
¾ tsp.	**(4 mL)**	**cinnamon**

Add:

¼ cup	**(50 mL)**	**chopped walnuts**

Cream until soft and creamy:

4 tbsp.	**(60 mL)**	**butter OR margarine, room temp.**
2 tbsp.	**(30 mL)**	**instant skim milk powder OR**
2 tsp.	**(10 mL)**	**noninstant skim milk powder**

Beat in until blended the cooked mixture and:

1	**(1)**	**large egg, beaten**
4 tbsp.	**(60 mL)**	**unsweetened concentrated orange juice, defrosted**

Mix in dry ingredients. Pour into a lightly buttered or oiled 8" (20 cm) square nonstick pan. Bake at 350°F (180°C) until done, 25 to 35 minutes. Cool 10 minutes on wire rack before removing from pan.

Serves 7-9.

DRIED APRICOT CAKE

Replace all the fruit in the Dried Fruit Fruitcake recipe with 18 dried apricots, finely chopped. Omit the chopped walnuts but add 1 tsp. (5 mL) almond extract to the creamed mixture.

CARROT CAKE

Sift together:

2 cups	**(500 mL)**	**sifted all-purpose flour**
2 tsp.	**(10 mL)**	**baking powder**
1 tsp.	**(5 mL)**	**baking soda**
1 tsp.	**(5 mL)**	**cinnamon**

Cream until soft and creamy:

½ cup	**(125 mL)**	**butter OR margarine, room temp.**
4 tbsp.	**(60 mL)**	**instant skim milk powder OR**
4 tsp.	**(20 mL)**	**noninstant skim milk powder**

Beat in:

2	**(2)**	**large eggs, well beaten**
2	**(2)**	**small ripe bananas, mashed with fork**
¾ cup	**(180 mL)**	**unsweetened concentrated orange juice, defrosted**
2 cups	**(500 mL)**	**grated raw carrots**

Add flour mixture. Mix just enough to blend. Pour into a buttered wax-paper-lined 9" (23 cm) tube pan. Bake at 350°F (180°C) until done, about 1 hour or until a cake tester comes out clean. Cool 10 minutes on wire rack. Unmould. Cool. Spread with:

Cheese Frosting, page 33

Serves 6-8. See photograph page 80A.

CARROT DATE CAKE

Cook and stir until thick and smooth; cool:

14	**(14)**	**pitted dates, chopped**
½ cup	**(125 mL)**	**unsweetened concentrated orange juice, defrosted**

Sift together:

1½ cups	**(375 mL)**	**sifted all-purpose flour**
2 tsp.	**(10 mL)**	**baking powder**
½ tsp.	**(2 mL)**	**baking soda**
1 tsp.	**(5 mL)**	**cinnamon**

CARROT DATE CAKE (continued)

Cream until soft and creamy:

6 tbsp.	**(90 mL)**	**butter OR margarine, room temp.**
2 tbsp.	**(30 mL)**	**instant skim milk powder OR**
2 tsp.	**(10 mL)**	**noninstant skim milk powder**

Beat in date mixture and:

1	**(1)**	**large egg, well beaten**
2 cups	**(500 mL)**	**grated raw carrots**

Stir in flour mixture, mixing just enough to blend. Batter is thick. Pour into a buttered wax-paper-lined 9" (23 cm) tube pan. Bake at 350°F (180°C) until firm, 45 to 55 minutes.

Serves 7-9.

DUTCH APPLE CAKE

Sift together:

1 cup	**(250 mL)**	**sifted all-purpose flour**
1½ tsp.	**(7 mL)**	**baking powder**
½ tsp.	**(2 mL)**	**baking soda**

Cut in with pastry blender until crumbly:

2 tbsp.	**(30 mL)**	**butter OR margarine,**

Beat together:

1	**(1)**	**large egg, well beaten**
½ cup	**(125 mL)**	**unsweetened concentrated apple juice**
½ tsp.	**(2 mL)**	**vanilla**

Add to dry ingredients. Mix just enough to moisten flour. Pour into lightly oiled 8" (20 cm) nonstick square pan.

Cut each quarter into 3 wedges:

3	**(3)**	**apples, peeled, cored, quartered**

Dip wedges in unsweetened concentrated apple juice, defrosted. Place in parallel rows with sharp edges pressed into batter. Sprinkle with a mixture of:

¼ tsp.	**(1 mL)**	**cinnamon**
¼ tsp.	**(1 mL)**	**nutmeg**

Bake at 350°F (180°C) until apples are tender, 35 to 40 minutes. Cut into squares. Serve hot with plain cream or whipped cream.

Serves 6-8.

COFFEE CAKE (With Crunchy Topping)

Sift together:

¾ cup	**(175 mL)**	**sifted all-purpose flour**
1½ tsp.	**(7 mL)**	**baking powder**
¼ tsp.	**(1 mL)**	**baking soda**
½ tsp.	**(2 mL)**	**cinnamon**

Cream until soft and creamy:

2 tbsp.	**(30 mL)**	**butter OR margarine, room temp.**
1 tbsp.	**(15 mL)**	**instant skim milk powder OR**
1¼ tsp.	**(6 mL)**	**noninstant skim milk powder**

Beat into creamed mixture:

1	**(1)**	**large egg, well beaten**
6 tbsp.	**(90 mL)**	**unsweetened concentrated orange juice**
½ tsp.	**(2 mL)**	**vanilla**

Stir into flour mixture. Mix only until blended. Pour into an oiled 8" (20 cm) nonstick square pan.

Combine well:

2 tbsp.	**(30 mL)**	**quick-cooking rolled oats**
4 tbsp.	**(60 mL)**	**unsweetened concentrated orange juice, defrosted**

Mix in:

⅓ cup	**(75 mL)**	**unsweetened shredded coconut**
⅓ cup	**(75 mL)**	**chopped pecans**
1 tbsp.	**(15 mL)**	**melted butter OR margarine**
½ tsp.	**(2 mL)**	**cinnamon**

Sprinkle evenly over batter. Bake 35 to 40 minutes at 350°F (180°C). Serve warm.

Serves 6-8.

COFFEE CAKE (With Streusel Topping)

Sprinkle evenly over Coffee Cake batter with a mixture of:

½ cup	**(125 mL)**	**fine dry cake OR cookie crumbs**
4 tsp.	**(20 mL)**	**melted butter OR margarine**
¼ tsp.	**(1 mL)**	**cinnamon**

PINEAPPLE UPSIDE-DOWN CAKE

Combine in a 9" (23 cm) round cake pan:

2 tbsp.	**(30 mL)**	**butter OR margarine, melted**
4 tbsp.	**(60 mL)**	**unsweetened concentrated pineapple juice, defrosted**
½ tsp.	**(2 mL)**	**almond extract**

Arrange 7 slices of canned pineapple to cover pan; insert 1 almond in centre of each slice.

Sift together:

1 cup	**(250 mL)**	**sifted all-purpose flour**
1 tsp.	**(5 mL)**	**baking powder**
½ tsp.	**(2 mL)**	**baking soda**

Cream until soft and creamy:

3 tbsp.	**(45 mL)**	**butter OR margarine, room temp.**
2 tbsp.	**(30 mL)**	**instant skim milk powder OR**
2 tsp.	**(10 mL)**	**noninstant skim milk powder**

Beat in:

1	**(1)**	**egg, well beaten**
6 tbsp.	**(90 mL)**	**unsweetened concentrated pineapple juice, defrosted**
½ tsp.	**(2 mL)**	**almond extract**

Add to flour mixture. Mix until blended. Pour over pineapple slices. Bake at 350°F (180°C) until well browned, 30 to 35 minutes. Invert onto serving dish. Cut into wedges. Serve hot with thin cream or any sweet sauce.

Serves 7.

APPLE UPSIDE-DOWN CAKE

Replace almond extract with vanilla and sliced pineapple with sliced apple. Slice 2 apples (peeled and cored) into 10 rings. Insert raisins in centre of each ring instead of an almond.

PINEAPPLE LAYER CAKE

Prepare Pineapple Filling, page 60.

Sift together:

1⅓ cups	**(325 mL)**	**sifted all-purpose flour**
2 tsp.	**(10 mL)**	**baking powder**
¼ tsp.	**(1 mL)**	**baking soda**

Cream until soft and creamy:

⅓ cup	**(75 mL)**	**butter OR margarine, room temp.**
2 tbsp.	**(30 mL)**	**instant skim milk powder OR**
2 tsp.	**(10 mL)**	**noninstant skim milk powder**

Beat in:

1	**(1)**	**large egg, well beaten**
⅔ cup	**(150 mL)**	**unsweetened concentrated pineapple juice, defrosted**
½ tsp.	**(2 mL)**	**almond extract**

Add to flour mixture. Mix just enough to blend. Pour into a lightly oiled 8" (20 cm) square nonstick pan. Bake at 350°F (180°C) until nicely browned, 25 to 30 minutes. Cool 10 minutes on wire rack before removing from pan. Split into 2 layers. Put layers together with Pineapple Filling. Spread top with:

Pineapple Topping, page 32

Serves 7-9.

ORANGE-LEMON JELLY ROLL

Prepare Orange-Lemon Filling, page 58.

Sift together:

¾ cup	**(175 mL)**	**sifted cake flour**
1¼ tsp.	**(6 mL)**	**baking powder**
¼ tsp.	**(1 mL)**	**baking soda**

Beat until stiff:

4	**(4)**	**egg whites, large**

Beat until thick:

4	**(4)**	**egg yolks, large**

ORANGE-LEMON JELLY ROLL (continued)

Beat into yolks:

2 tbsp. (30 mL) unsweetened concentrated orange juice, defrosted
½ tsp. (2 mL) lemon extract

Add yolk mixture to egg whites; beat to combine. Fold in flour mixture. Spread evenly in lightly oiled nonstick baking sheet. Bake at 350°F (180°C) until browned, 15-18 minutes. Turn out quickly onto wax paper; trim off edges; roll up with wax paper inside. Cool. Unroll. Spread with cooled filling. Roll up again. Slice and serve or, if desired, serve with a sweet sauce.

Serves 8-10.

BAKED ALASKA

Cut 6 servings of:

Jelly Roll OR any cake

If plain OR sponge cake is used, spread with any:

Jam, pages 96-99

Place on each a scoop of:

Ice Cream, page 57

Freeze.

Make meringue by beating until stiff:

4 (4) egg whites

Add and beat until blended:

½ tsp. (2 mL) cream of tartar
¾ tsp. (4 mL) cornstarch
3 tbsp. (45 mL) unsweetened concentrated fruit juice, defrosted

Cover ice cream and cake completely with meringue. Bake at 450°F (230°C) until lightly browned, about 4 minutes. Serve at once.

Serves 6.

Frostings and Toppings

WHIPPED CREAM

Beat until peaks form:

½ cup	**(125 mL)**	**whipping cream**

Add and beat until blended:

½ tsp.	**(2 mL)**	**unsweetened concentrated fruit juice, defrosted**

Be careful to avoid overbeating.

Yields about 1 cup (250 mL).

MOCK WHIPPED CREAM

Blend until smooth and fluffy:

1 cup	**(250 mL)**	**cottage cheese**
2 tbsp.	**(30 mL)**	**milk**
1 tbsp.	**(15 mL)**	**soft butter OR margarine**
1 tbsp.	**(15 mL)**	**unsweetened concentrated fruit juice, defrosted**
¼ tsp.	**(1 mL)**	**vanilla**

Makes 1⅓ cups (325 mL).

LOW-CALORIE WHIPPED CREAM

Combine:

2 tbsp.	**(30 mL)**	**hot water**
1 tsp.	**(5 mL)**	**gelatine**

Add and stir until dissolved:

1 cup	**(250 mL)**	**evaporated skim milk, hot**

Chill until it thickens slightly, then add:

2 tbsp.	**(30 mL)**	**unsweetened concentrated fruit juice**
¼ tsp.	**(1 mL)**	**vanilla**

Beat until light and fluffy. At its best when used immediately, but will keep for several days.

Makes about 2 cups (500 mL).

LOW-CALORIE WHIPPED TOPPING

Combine:

1 tbsp.	**(15 mL)**	**hot water**
½ tsp.	**(2 mL)**	**gelatine**

Add and stir until dissolved:

6 tbsp.	**(90 mL)**	**hot unsweetened fruit juice**

Chill until it thickens slightly, then add:

3 tbsp.	**(45 mL)**	**noninstant skim milk powder OR**
½ cup	**(125 mL)**	**instant skim milk powder**
¼ tsp.	**(1 mL)**	**vanilla**

Beat until stiff and glossy.

Makes about 1¾ cups (425 mL).

WHIPPED ORANGE TOPPING

Beat on high until peaks form:

⅓ cup	**(75 mL)**	**unsweetened orange juice, chilled**
¼ tsp.	**(1 mL)**	**grated orange rind**
1 tbsp.	**(15 mL)**	**lemon juice**
3 tbsp.	**(45 mL)**	**noninstant skim milk powder OR**
½ cup	**(125 mL)**	**instant skim milk powder**

Best used at once.

Makes about 1¾ cups (425 mL).

PINEAPPLE TOPPING

Stand container in hot water until dissolved:

½ pkg.	**(½ pkg.)**	**gelatine**
4 tbsp.	**(60 mL)**	**unsweetened concentrated pineapple juice, defrosted**

Stir in and then chill until partially set:

½ cup	**(125 mL)**	**juice drained from crushed pineapple**

Cover top of cake with:

¾ cup	**(175 mL)**	**canned unsweetened crushed pineapple, well drained**

Spread gelatine mixture over pineapple. Chill.

Will cover a 9" (23 cm) square cake.

APPLE-CHEESE TOPPING

Cook and stir until apples are tender; cool:

3	**(3)**	**medium apples, peeled, sliced**
3 tbsp.	**(45 mL)**	**unsweetened concentrated apple juice, defrosted**
1 tbsp.	**(15 mL)**	**lemon juice**

Beat until fluffy:

2 tbsp.	**(30 mL)**	**cream cheese, room temp.**

Beat in apple mixture.

Will cover a 9" (23 cm) cake.

PINEAPPLE-CHEESE FROSTING

Beat until fluffy:

8.8 oz.	**(250 g)**	**cream cheese, cubed, room temp.**

Blend until a bit chunky:

2	**(2)**	**slices, canned, unsweetened pineapple**

Add to cream cheese and beat until blended.

Will frost a 9" (23 cm) cake.

Custard Fruit Flan, page 21

CREAM CHEESE FROSTING

Beat until smooth and fluffy:

8.8 oz.	**(250 g)**	**cream cheese, cubed, room temp.**
2 tbsp.	**(30 mL)**	**unsweetened concentrated fruit juice, defrosted**

Will frost a 9" (23 cm) cake.

See photograph page 80A.

COTTAGE CHEESE FROSTING

Blend until smooth:

1 cup	**(250 mL)**	**cottage cheese**
1 tbsp.	**(15 mL)**	**unsweetened concentrated fruit juice, defrosted**
½	**(½)**	**ripe banana, mashed with fork**

Will frost a 9" (23 cm) cake.

CAROB FROSTING

Cook on low until smooth:

8	**(8)**	**pitted dates, chopped**
3 tbsp.	**(45 mL)**	**unsweetened concentrated apple juice, defrosted**

Combine in saucepan the blended mixture and:

3 tbsp.	**(45 mL)**	**noninstant skim milk powder**
½ cup	**(125 mL)**	**sifted carob powder**
2 tbsp.	**(30 mL)**	**unsweetened concentrated apple juice, defrosted**
1 tbsp.	**(15 mL)**	**butter OR margarine, melted**

Simmer and stir until thick and smooth.

Add:

1 tsp.	**(5 mL)**	**vanilla**

Cool.

Will frost an 8" (20 cm) cake.

SEVEN-MINUTE FROSTING

Beat in top part of double boiler until blended:

2	**(2)**	**egg whites**
5 tbsp.	**(75 mL)**	**unsweetened concentrated fruit juice**

Cook and beat over boiling water until peaks form, about 7 minutes.

Beat in:

1 tsp.	**(5 mL)**	**vanilla**
1 tsp.	**(5 mL)**	**baking powder**

Will frost a 9" (23 cm) cake generously.

BUTTERY ICING

Beat at high speed until smooth and creamy:

4 tbsp.	**(60 mL)**	**butter, room temp.**
4 tsp.	**(20 mL)**	**noninstant skim milk powder**

Add and beat until blended:

2 tbsp.	**(30 mL)**	**unsweetened concentrated fruit juice**
2 tbsp.	**(30 mL)**	**any jam, pages 96 to 99**

Will cover a 9" (23 cm) cake.

MERINGUE

Beat until soft peaks form:

2	**(2)**	**egg whites**

Add and beat until stiff:

½ tsp.	**(2 mL)**	**cornstarch**
¼ tsp.	**(1 mL)**	**cream of tartar**

Beat in:

2 tbsp.	**(30 mL)**	**unsweetened concentrated fruit juice**

Swirl decoratively over pie filling or on top of cake. Bake at 325°F (160°C) until a delicate brown, 15 to 20 minutes.

Make sure that meringue touches the pie crust at all points or it will pull away during baking. Cool away from drafts, to prevent shrinking.

Will cover a 9" (23 cm) pie or cake.

ORANGE MERINGUE

Replace the unsweetened concentrated fruit juice in the Meringue with unsweetened concentrated orange juice and ½ tsp. (2 mL) grated orange rind.

BROILED APPLESAUCE MERINGUE

Beat until soft peaks form:

1	**(1)**	**egg white**

Add and beat until stiff:

½ tsp.	**(2 mL)**	**cornstarch**
⅛ tsp.	**(0.5 mL)**	**baking powder**

Mix together:

½ cup	**(125 mL)**	**applesauce**
2 tbsp.	**(30 mL)**	**unsweetened concentrated apple juice, defrosted**

Fold into egg white. Pile unevenly on top of cake. Broil until lightly browned.

Will cover a 8" (20 cm) cake.

BROILED BANANA MERINGUE

Replace the applesauce in the Broiled Applesauce Meringue with 1 large ripe banana. Mash the banana with a fork before mixing with the unsweetened concentrated apple juice.

TO DIVIDE AN EGG:

Beat an egg in a measuring cup. Divide according to the amount measured in the cup.

Cookies, Bars Squares and Turnovers

SPICY APPLE COOKIES

Cook and stir until juice has evaporated; mash; cool:

6 tbsp.	**(90 mL)**	**unsweetened concentrated apple juice, defrosted**
1	**(1)**	**large apple, peeled, sliced**

Sift together:

1⅓ cups	**(325 mL)**	**sifted all-purpose flour**
1 tsp.	**(5 mL)**	**baking powder**
¾ tsp.	**(4 mL)**	**baking soda**
1 tsp.	**(5 mL)**	**cinnamon**
½ tsp.	**(2 mL)**	**ginger**
½ tsp.	**(2 mL)**	**nutmeg**
pinch	**(pinch)**	**cloves**

Cut in with pastry blender until mixture resembles fine crumbs:

½ cup	**(125 mL)**	**butter OR margarine**

Combine apple mixture with:

¼ cup	**(50 mL)**	**mashed ripe banana, mash with fork**

Mix in dry ingredients. Drop from spoon onto a lightly oiled cookie sheet. Flatten with tines of fork. Bake at 375°F (190°C) until golden brown, about 20 minutes.

Makes 30.

FOR EASE IN MAKING DROP COOKIES:

Use a lightly oiled spoon in making drop cookies. The batter will slip off readily.

PEANUT BUTTER COOKIES

Sift together:

1¼ cups	**(300 mL)**	**sifted all-purpose flour**
¾ tsp.	**(4 mL)**	**baking powder**
¾ tsp.	**(4 mL)**	**baking soda**

Cream well:

3 tbsp.	**(45 mL)**	**butter OR shortening, room temp.**
⅔ cup	**(150 mL)**	**peanut butter**

Add to peanut butter mixture, beating until blended:

⅓ cup	**(75 mL)**	**mashed ripe banana, mash with fork**
2 tbsp.	**(30 mL)**	**unsweetened concentrated fruit juice**
½ tsp.	**(2 mL)**	**almond extract**

Stir into flour mixture. Knead well. Shape into 2 rolls, 1½" (4 cm) diameter. Wrap in plastic wrap. Chill 2 hours or overnight. Slice rolls ⅛" (3 mm) thick. Place on lightly oiled cookie sheet. Bake at 350°F (180°C) until golden brown, 12 to 15 minutes.

Makes about 34.

COCONUT COOKIES

Mix until blended:

4 tbsp.	**(60 mL)**	**unsweetened concentrated orange juice**
¾ cup	**(175 mL)**	**quick-cooking rolled oats**

Sift together:

½ cup	**(125 mL)**	**sifted all-purpose flour**
1 tsp.	**(5 mL)**	**baking powder**
¼ tsp.	**(1 mL)**	**baking soda**

Cut in with pastry blender until mixture resembles fine crumbs:

5 tbsp.	**(75 mL)**	**butter OR margarine**

Beat into rolled oat mixture:

⅓ cup	**(75 mL)**	**mashed ripe banana, mash with fork**
½ cup	**(125 mL)**	**unsweetened toasted shredded coconut**

Stir in flour mixture. Drop from spoon onto a lightly oiled cookie sheet. Flatten with fork. Bake at 350°F (180°C) until golden, 20 minutes.

Makes 40.

DATE COOKIES

Bring to a boil, then reduce to low:

4 tbsp.	**(60 mL)**	**unsweetened concentrated orange juice, defrosted**
¾ cup	**(175 mL)**	**pitted dates, chopped**

Simmer and stir until smooth and thick. Cool.

Sift together:

1 cup	**(250 mL)**	**sifted all-purpose flour**
1 tsp.	**(5 mL)**	**baking powder**
½ tsp.	**(2 mL)**	**baking soda**
½ tsp.	**(2 mL)**	**cinnamon**

Cut in with pastry blender until mixture resembles fine crumbs:

6 tbsp.	**(90 mL)**	**shortening OR butter, cold**

Stir in cooled mixture and:

¼ cup	**(50 mL)**	**chopped nuts**

Knead well. Gather dough into a ball. Roll out ⅛" (3 mm) thick. Cut with a 2½" (6.5 cm) cookie cutter or tumbler. Gather the scraps of dough. Roll and cut again until all is used. Place on cookie sheet. Bake at 350°F (180°C) until nicely browned, 12 to 15 minutes.

Makes about 30.

APRICOT JAM COOKIES

Sift together:

1 cup	**(250 mL)**	**sifted all-purpose flour**
½ tsp.	**(2 mL)**	**baking powder**
½ tsp.	**(2 mL)**	**baking soda**

Cut in with pastry blender until mixture resembles fine crumbs:

6 tbsp.	**(90 mL)**	**butter OR shortening, cold**

Mix together then sprinkle over flour mixture:

2 tbsp.	**(30 mL)**	**unsweetened concentrated orange juice, defrosted**
½ tsp.	**(2 mL)**	**almond extract**

APRICOT JAM COOKIES (continued)

Toss with fork just until flour is moistened. Knead slightly. Shape into balls, 1¼" (3.2 cm) in diameter. Place on cookie sheet. Flatten a little. Dent centres with handle of wooden spoon. Bake 6 minutes at 350°F (180°C), dent centres again and bake 10 to 15 minutes. Cool. Fill centres with:

Apricot Jam, page 96

Makes about 14. See photograph on back cover.

CAROB COOKIES

Bring to a boil, then simmer and stir until smooth and thick; cool:

½ cup	**(125 mL)**	**pitted dates, chopped**
3 tbsp.	**(45 mL)**	**unsweetened concentrated fruit juice, defrosted**

Sift together:

¾ cup	**(175 mL)**	**sifted all-purpose flour**
½ tsp.	**(2 mL)**	**baking powder**
½ tsp.	**(2 mL)**	**baking soda**
3 tbsp.	**(45 mL)**	**carob powder**

Cut in with pastry blender until it resembles fine crumbs:

5 tbsp.	**(75 mL)**	**butter OR shortening, cold**

Mix date mixture with:

1 tsp.	**(5 mL)**	**vanilla**

Combine with dry ingredients; mix well. Form into balls; place on cookie sheet; flatten to ⅛" (3 mm) with tines of fork. Bake at 375°F (190°C) for 15 to 18 minutes.

Makes about 20.

COCONUT MACAROONS

Beat until peaks form:

2	**(2)**	**egg whites**

Add and beat until stiff:

½ tsp.	**(2 mL)**	**vanilla**
¼ tsp.	**(1 mL)**	**cream of tartar**

Combine, cook and stir until thick and clear:

2 tsp.	**(10 mL)**	**cornstarch**
5 tbsp.	**(75 mL)**	**unsweetened concentrated apple juice, defrosted**
2 tbsp.	**(30 mL)**	**water**

Gradually beat into egg white mixture until well blended.

Fold in:

1¼ cups	**(300 mL)**	**unsweetened shredded coconut**

Drop by spoonfuls onto oiled cookie sheet. Bake at 300°F (150°C) until light brown, about 20 minutes. Leave in oven for 20 minutes with heat turned off and door slightly opened.

Makes 30.

VARIATION:

PEANUT MACAROONS: Replace coconut with finely chopped peanuts.

CREAM CHEESE COOKIES

Sift together:

1 cup	**(250 mL)**	**sifted all-purpose flour**
½ tsp.	**(2 mL)**	**baking powder**

Cream well:

¼ lb.	**(115 g)**	**cream cheese, room temp.**
¼ lb.	**(115 g)**	**butter OR shortening, room temp.**
½ tsp.	**(2 mL)**	**unsweetened concentrated fruit juice**

Add flour mixture and cut in until it resembles fine crumbs. Knead well. Shape into 2 balls. Wrap in plastic wrap. Chill 2 hours or overnight. Roll each ball into a circle ⅛" (3 mm) thick. Cut it into 8 wedges. Spread each wedge with jam. Roll from wide end. Place tip end down on cookie sheet. Bake at 375°F (190°C) until lightly browned, about 20 minutes.

Makes 16.

WHEAT GERM COOKIES

Combine:

⅔ cup	**(150 mL)**	**wheat germ, preferably raw**
¾ cup	**(175 mL)**	**whole-wheat flour**
1½ tsp.	**(7 mL)**	**baking powder**
½ tsp.	**(2 mL)**	**baking soda**
¾ tsp.	**(4 mL)**	**cinnamon**

Cut in until it resembles fine crumbs:

½ cup	**(125 mL)**	**butter OR margarine**

Add:

¼ cup	**(50 mL)**	**raisins**
¼ cup	**(50 mL)**	**nuts, finely chopped**

Mix together and stir into flour mixture:

⅓ cup	**(75 mL)**	**mashed ripe banana, mash with fork**
2 tbsp.	**(30 mL)**	**unsweetened concentrated orange juice, defrosted**

Drop from spoon onto a lightly oiled cookie sheet. Flatten with tines of fork. Bake at 350°F (180°C) until brown, 15 to 20 minutes.

Makes about 35.

DATE OR RAISIN TURNOVERS

Roll to ⅛" (3 mm) thick:

Two-Crust Pie Pastry, page 5 or 6

Cut into 4" (10 cm) squares or rounds. Place on each a rounded:

1 tsp.	**(5 mL)**	**Date Filling, page 60 OR Raisin Filling, page 61**

Moisten pastry edges with milk. Fold to form triangles, if cut in squares; semicircles, if cut in rounds. Press edges with tines of fork to seal. Prick tops to allow steam to escape. Place on cookie sheet. Brush tops with milk. Bake at 425°F (220°C) until a delicate brown, 12 to 15 minutes.

Makes 14.

JAM-FILLED OATMEAL COOKIES

Sift together:

1¼ cups	**(300 mL)**	**sifted all-purpose flour**
¾ tsp.	**(4 mL)**	**baking powder**
¾ tsp.	**(4 mL)**	**baking soda**
1 tsp.	**(5 mL)**	**cinnamon**

Add:

1¼ cups	**(300 mL)**	**quick-cooking rolled oats**

Cut in with pastry blender until mixture resembles fine crumbs:

½ cup	**(125 mL)**	**butter OR shortening, cold**

Beat together and mix into flour mixture:

1	**(1)**	**egg, beaten**
3 tbsp.	**(45 mL)**	**unsweetened concentrated orange juice, defrosted**

Chill 1 hour. Roll dough ⅛" (3 mm) thick. Cut with 2" (5 cm) cookie cutter. Bake on a lightly oiled cookie sheet at 350°F (180°C) until brown, 12 to 15 minutes. Serve by spreading, between 2 cookies, with:

Jam, pages 96 to 99

Makes 24.

PINEAPPLE COCONUT BARS

Prepare Pineapple Filling, page 60.

Sift together:

1 cup	**(250 mL)**	**sifted all-purpose flour**
½ tsp.	**(2 mL)**	**baking powder**
½ tsp.	**(2 mL)**	**baking soda**

Cut in with pastry blender until mixture resembles fine crumbs:

3 tbsp.	**(45 mL)**	**butter OR margarine**

Beat together:

1	**(1)**	**large egg yolk**
4 tbsp.	**(60 mL)**	**unsweetened pineapple juice**

Stir in flour mixture. Pour into a lightly buttered or oiled 8" (20 cm) square nonstick pan. Press. Bake 15 minutes at 350°F (180°C). Spread Pineapple Filling on baked pastry.

PINEAPPLE COCONUT BARS (continued)

Beat until stiff:

1	**(1)**	**large egg white**

Beat in until blended:

¼ tsp.	**(1 mL)**	**cornstarch**
⅛ tsp.	**(0.5 mL)**	**cream of tartar**
1 tbsp.	**(15 mL)**	**unsweetened concentrated pineapple juice**

Fold in:

½ cup	**(125 mL)**	**toasted shredded coconut**

Spread on pineapple filling. Bake at 325°F (160°C) until a delicate brown, 15 to 20 minutes. Cut into bars, 1" X 2½" (2.5 cm X 6.5 cm).

Makes 24. See photograph on back cover.

JAM BARS

Sift together:

¾ cup	**(175 mL)**	**sifted all-purpose flour**
½ tsp.	**(2 mL)**	**baking powder**
½ tsp.	**(2 mL)**	**baking soda**

Add:

¾ cup	**(175 mL)**	**quick-cooking rolled oats**

Cut in with pastry blender until crumbly:

5 tbsp.	**(75 mL)**	**butter OR margarine**

Mix in:

⅓ cup	**(75 mL)**	**toasted shredded coconut**

Sprinkle:

2 tbsp.	**(30 mL)**	**unsweetened concentrated fruit juice, defrosted**

Toss with fork until flour and oats are moistened. Reserve ⅔ cup (150 mL) and pat remainder on lightly oiled 8" (20 cm) square nonstick pan. Spread generously with any:

Jam, pages 96 to 99

Sprinkle reserved mixture over jam. Bake at 350°F (180°C) until brown, 25 to 30 minutes. Cut into bars, 1" X 2½" (2.5 cm X 6.5 cm).

Makes 24. See photograph on back cover.

FIG BARS

Prepare Fig Filling, page 60. Sift together:

2 cups	**(500 mL)**	**sifted all-purpose flour**
¾ tsp.	**(4 mL)**	**baking powder**
¾ tsp.	**(4 mL)**	**baking soda**

Cream until soft and creamy:

½ cup	**(125 mL)**	**butter OR shortening, room temp.**

Beat in:

1	**(1)**	**egg, beaten**
2 tbsp.	**(30 mL)**	**unsweetened concentrated orange juice**
½ tsp.	**(2 mL)**	**vanilla**

Add flour mixture. Mix well. Roll dough into an oblong 12" X 16" (30 cm X 40 cm). Divide into 3 strips, 4" X 16" (10 cm X 40 cm). Spread fig filling along the centre length of each strip. Fold edges to lap just over the centre, moistening 1 edge. Press lightly to seal. Cut in 1¾" (4.4 cm) lengths. Lift gently onto oiled cookie sheet with spatula. Brush tops with milk. Bake at 400°F (200°C) until a light brown, 12 to 15 minutes.

Makes 27.

DATE SQUARES

Prepare Date Filling, page 60. Sift together:

1 cup	**(250 mL)**	**sifted all-purpose flour**
½ tsp.	**(2 mL)**	**baking powder**
½ tsp.	**(2 mL)**	**baking soda**

Add:

1½ cups	**(375 mL)**	**quick-cooking rolled oats**

Cut in with pastry blender until crumbly:

½ cup	**(125 mL)**	**butter OR margarine**

Sprinkle:

3 tbsp.	**(45 mL)**	**unsweetened concentrated orange juice**

Mix well. Pat half of crumb mixture on a lightly oiled 8" (20 cm) square nonstick pan. Spread with Date Filling. Pat remaining mixture on top. Bake at 350°F (180°C) until golden, 35 to 40 minutes. Cut into squares.

Serves 7-9.

Desserts: Baked, Fruit and Cold

BLUEBERRY COBBLER

Combine in a saucepan:

2 tbsp.	**(30 mL)**	**all-purpose flour**
4 tbsp.	**(60 mL)**	**warm water**

Add:

½ cup	**(125 mL)**	**unsweetened concentrated orange juice, defrosted**
½ tsp.	**(2 mL)**	**vanilla**
3 cups	**(750 mL)**	**blueberries**

Cook and stir until boiling. Turn off heat. Cover to keep warm.

Sift together:

1 cup	**(250 mL)**	**sifted all-purpose flour**
1¼ tsp.	**(6 mL)**	**baking powder**
½ tsp.	**(2 mL)**	**baking soda**

Combine:

⅔ cup	**(150 mL)**	**unsweetened fruit juice**
2 tbsp.	**(30 mL)**	**vegetable oil**

Add to flour mixture. Mix just enough to blend. Pour blueberry mixture into a buttered 1½-quart (1.5 L) casserole. Spread batter over mixture. Bake at 425°F (220°C) until browned, about 30 minutes. Serve warm with whipped cream.

Serves 6.

APPLE CRISP

Cook and stir 10 minutes; turn off heat; cover to keep warm:

⅓ cup	**(75 mL)**	**unsweetened apple juice**
6	**(6)**	**medium cooking apples, peeled, sliced**

Combine:

2 tbsp.	**(30 mL)**	**sunflower seeds**
2 tbsp.	**(30 mL)**	**quick-cooking rolled oats**
2 tbsp.	**(30 mL)**	**wheat germ, preferably raw**
3 tbsp.	**(45 mL)**	**unsweetened concentrated apple juice**

Mix in:

4 tbsp.	**(60 mL)**	**fine cracker crumbs**
½ tsp.	**(2 mL)**	**cinnamon**
2 tbsp.	**(30 mL)**	**peanut oil**

Pour hot apples into a buttered 6-cup (1.5 L) baking dish. Sprinkle with crumb mixture. Bake at 350°F (180°C) until brown, 35 to 45 minutes.

Serves 6.

APPLESAUCE

Cook and stir until apples are tender, about 15 minutes:

4	**(4)**	**medium apples, peeled, cored, sliced**
⅓ cup	**(75 mL)**	**water**
1 tbsp.	**(15 mL)**	**lemon juice**

Serve hot or cold.

Serves 4.

BAKED APPLES

Place in baking dish:

¾ cup	**(175 mL)**	**unsweetened apple juice**
4	**(4)**	**medium apples, cored, peeled ⅓ down**
		raisins (optional) to fill apples

Sprinkle on each a few grains of cinnamon and nutmeg.

Baste during baking at 15 minute intervals. Bake at 375°F (190°C) until apples are tender, about 45 minutes.

Serves 4.

CREAM PUFFS

Heat in saucepan until boiling; reduce heat to medium:

1 cup (250 mL) water
½ cup (125 mL) butter OR margarine

Dump in, all at once:

1 cup (250 mL) sifted all-purpose flour

Stir vigorously until mixture forms a ball around spoon. Remove from heat.

Beat in thoroughly, 1 at a time:

4 (4) eggs

Beat until mixture is thick, shiny and does not adhere to spoon. Drop from tablespoon 2" (5 cm) apart onto cookie sheet, shaping in round cone-like forms. Bake 15 minutes at 400°F (200°C) reduce to 325°F (160°C) for 25 minutes. Slit each puff in 1 of the natural divisions made by baking. Cool. Fill puffs through the slits, with any of the fillings listed below.

Makes 12.

ECLAIRS

Shape Cream Puff batter, with pastry bag using a plain tube, into strips 1" (2.5 cm) wide and 4" (10 cm) long. Bake as for Cream Puffs. Cool, split and fill with any of the fillings listed below. Frost with:

Carob Frosting, page 33

Makes 12.

* FILL CREAM PUFFS OR ECLAIRS WITH ANY OF THE FOLLOWING:

Whipped Cream, page 30
Mock Whipped Cream, page 30
Custard or Custard Cream Filling, page 59
Cream Filling, page 58
Cottage Cheese Filling, page 59

ORANGE-LEMON CHEESECAKE

Mix together:

1 cup	**(250 mL)**	**fine crumbs (see page 8)**
4 tbsp.	**(60 mL)**	**melted butter OR margarine**
½ tsp.	**(2 mL)**	**cinnamon (optional)**

Press ¾ of mixture into bottom of 9" (23 cm) springform pan.

Place in blender and blend until smooth:

2	**(2)**	**egg yolks**
2 tbsp.	**(30 mL)**	**flour**
4 tbsp.	**(60 mL)**	**evaporated milk**
		thin rind of ½ of a lemon
		thin rind of ¼ of an orange
1 tbsp.	**(15 mL)**	**lemon juice**
¾ cup	**(175 mL)**	**unsweetened concentrated orange juice, defrosted**
1 cup	**(250 mL)**	**cottage cheese (first amount)**

Add gradually, blending again until smooth:

1 cup	**(250 mL)**	**cottage cheese (second amount)**

Beat on high until stiff:

2	**(2)**	**egg whites**

Fold together egg whites and blended mixture. Pour into crumb crust. Sprinkle with remaining crumbs. Bake at 325°F (160°C) until centre is firm, 45 to 55 minutes. Chill at least 2 hours. Remove rim of springform pan before serving.

Serves 6.

STEWED PRUNES

Soak overnight:

18	**(18)**	**prunes**
1 cup	**(250 mL)**	**water**

Add; bring to a boil, reduce heat:

2	**(2)**	**slices of orange OR lemon, cut crosswise**

Simmer until tender, 10 minutes. Serve hot or cold.

Serves 3.

STEWED FIGS

Soak overnight:

12	**(12)**	**figs**
1½ cups	**(375 mL)**	**water**

Add; bring to a boil, reduce heat:

2	**(2)**	**slices lemon, cut crosswise**

Simmer until tender, 10 minutes. Serve hot or cold.

Serves 3-4.

PRUNE WHIP

Combine:

1½ cups	**(375 mL)**	**prune pulp (blend cooked prunes in blender)**
3 tbsp.	**(45 mL)**	**unsweetened concentrated orange juice, defrosted**

Fold into:

3	**(3)**	**egg whites, stiffly beaten**

Chill and serve or bake at 350°F (180°C) until firm, 35 to 45 minutes.

Serves 4-5.

FRUIT WHIP

Replace prune pulp in the Prune Whip with any cooked fruit pulp, crushed strawberries or any other crushed raw fruit.

ORANGE JELLY

Stand container in hot water until dissolved:

1 tbsp.	**(15 mL)**	**gelatine**
¼ cup	**(50 mL)**	**unsweetened orange juice**

Stir into:

1¾ cups	**(425 mL)**	**unsweetened orange juice**

Spoon into dessert dishes. Chill until set.

Serves 4.

GRAPE OR PINEAPPLE JELLY

Replace unsweetened orange juice in the Orange Jelly recipe with unsweetened grape OR pineapple juice.

LEMON JELLY

Stand container in hot water until dissolved:

1 tbsp.	**(15 mL)**	**gelatine**
4 tbsp.	**(60 mL)**	**unsweetened concentrated apple juice, defrosted**

Stir into:

1½ cups	**(375 mL)**	**unsweetened pineapple juice**
2 tbsp.	**(30 mL)**	**lemon juice**
		grated rind of ½ a lemon

Spoon into dessert dishes. Chill until set.

Serves 3.

RASPBERRY JELLY

Stand container in hot water until dissolved:

1 tbsp.	**(15 mL)**	**gelatine**
¼ cup	**(50 mL)**	**unsweetened red grape juice**

Stir into:

¾ cup	**(175 mL)**	**unsweetened red grape juice**
1 cup	**(250 mL)**	**strained, mashed raspberries**

Spoon into dessert dishes. Chill until set.

Serves 4.

JELLY WHIP

Prepare any Jelly Recipe, page 50, 51. Chill until partially set. Whip until light and frothy. Pour into a mould or dessert dishes. Chill until set.

Serves 4-5.

YOGURT JELLY WHIP

Fold into Jelly Whip, 1 cup (250 mL) plain yogurt. Spoon into 6 dessert dishes. Chill until set.

Serves 6.

JELLIED PINEAPPLE

Stand container in hot water until dissolved:

1 tbsp.	**(15 mL)**	**gelatine**
¼ cup	**(50 mL)**	**unsweetened pineapple juice**

Stir into:

1⅔ cups	**(400 mL)**	**unsweetened pineapple juice**
1 cup	**(250 mL)**	**well-drained, unsweetened crushed pineapple**

Chill until partially set. Mix to distribute pineapple evenly. Chill until set.

Serves 5-6.

FRESH FRUITS IN JELLY

Stand container in hot water until dissolved:

1 tbsp.	**(15 mL)**	**gelatine**
5 tbsp.	**(75 mL)**	**unsweetened fruit juice**

Stir into:

1⅔ cups	**(400 mL)**	**unsweetened mixed fruit juice**

Pour ⅔ cup (150 mL) into a mould. Chill until set. Arrange a layer of:

sliced banana

Add another ⅔ cup (150 mL) gelatine mixture. Chill until set. Arrange a layer of:

sliced strawberries

Add remainder of gelatine mixture. Chill until set. **NOTE:** Any 2 kinds of fruit may be used. Fresh pineapple must be cooked until tender or jelly will not set.

Serves 6. See photograph page 16A.

LOW-CALORIE FRUIT BAVARIAN

Stand container in hot water until dissolved:

1 tbsp.	**(15 mL)**	**gelatine**
4 tbsp.	**(60 mL)**	**unsweetened concentrated apple juice, defrosted**

Stir in and then chill until partially set:

1 cup	**(250 mL)**	**fruit pulp***
1 cup	**(250 mL)**	**unsweetened pineapple juice**
1 tbsp.	**(15 mL)**	**lemon juice**

Add and beat until it doubles in volume:

⅔ cup	**(150 mL)**	**instant skim milk powder OR**
4 tbsp.	**(60 mL)**	**noninstant skim milk powder**

Pour into a mould. Chill until set.

Serves 6.

* FRUIT PULP:

Mash or blend until smooth, cooked fruits, fresh apricots, nectarines, crushed strawberries or raspberries.

FRUIT BAVARIAN

Replace skim milk powder in Low-Calorie Fruit Bavarian with ¾ cup (175 mL) whipped cream. Beat gelatine mixture until light and frothy. Fold into whipped cream. Pour into a mould. Chill until set.

Serves 6.

LOW-CALORIE LEMON BAVARIAN

Stand container in hot water until dissolved:

1 tbsp.	**(15 mL)**	**gelatine**
4 tbsp.	**(60 mL)**	**unsweetened concentrated apple juice, defrosted**

Stir in and then chill until partially set:

2 tbsp.	**(30 mL)**	**lemon juice**
¼ tsp.	**(1 mL)**	**grated lemon rind**
⅔ cup	**(150 mL)**	**unsweetened pineapple juice**

Pour into bowl and place in freezer until crystals form:

1 cup	**(250 mL)**	**evaporated skim milk**

Beat evaporated milk until thick and fluffy. Beat partially set gelatine until light and frothy. Fold the 2 mixtures together. Pour into a mould. Chill until set.

Serves 4-6.

APPLE SNOW

Stand container in hot water until dissolved:

6 tbsp.	**(90 mL)**	**unsweetened apple juice**
2 tsp.	**(10 mL)**	**gelatine**

Stir in and then chill until partially thickened:

1 cup	**(250 mL)**	**applesauce**

Beat until stiff:

1	**(1)**	**egg white**

Beat in gelatine mixture until light and frothy. Pour into a mould. Chill until set.

Serves 4.

NO-BAKE PINEAPPLE CHEESECAKE

Mix well; press into a 9" (23 cm) springform pan; chill:

¾ cup	**(175 mL)**	**fine crumbs (see page 8)**
3 tbsp.	**(45 mL)**	**melted butter OR margarine**

Stand container in hot water until dissolved:

1 tbsp.	**(15 mL)**	**gelatine**
3 tbsp.	**(45 mL)**	**water**
5 tbsp.	**(75 mL)**	**unsweetened concentrated pineapple juice**

Stir into:

1 tbsp.	**(15 mL)**	**lemon juice**
1¼ cups	**(300 mL)**	**unsweetened pineapple juice**

Beat until light and fluffy:

1 lb.	**(454 g)**	**cream cheese, cubed, room temp.**

Gradually beat in gelatine mixture. Chill until partially set.

Beat into partially set mixture until volume doubles:

1 cup	**(250 mL)**	**instant skim milk powder OR**
6 tbsp.	**(90 mL)**	**noninstant skim milk powder**

Fold in:

¾ cup	**(175 mL)**	**well-drained, unsweetened crushed pineapple**

Pour over crumb mixture. Chill until firm.

Serves 6-8.

QUICK BANANA DESSERT

Beat until thick and smooth:

3 tbsp.	**(45 mL)**	**noninstant skim milk powder OR**
½ cup	**(125 mL)**	**instant skim milk powder**
½ cup	**(125 mL)**	**unsweetened pineapple juice**
1 tsp.	**(5 mL)**	**unsweetened concentrated apple juice**
¼ tsp.	**(1 mL)**	**banana extract**

Fold in gently:

3	**(3)**	**sliced ripe bananas**

Spoon into pedestal dessert glasses. Serve at once.

Serves 5-6.

ORANGE BLANC MANGE

Combine in top part of double boiler until smooth:

4 tbsp.	**(60 mL)**	**cornstarch**
½ cup	**(125 mL)**	**milk**

Add, stir and cook over boiling water until thick:

1¾ cups	**(425 mL)**	**milk, hot**

Mix in:

¾ cup	**(175 mL)**	**unsweetened concentrated orange juice, defrosted**

Pour into 5 dessert dishes. Cool. Garnish with:

Whipped Cream, page 30

Serves 5.

VARIATIONS:

PINEAPPLE BLANC MANGE: Replace unsweetened concentrated orange juice with unsweetened concentrated pineapple juice.

ORANGE OR PINEAPPLE CUSTARD BLANC MANGE: Add 2 beaten eggs to Orange or Pineapple Blanc Mange by pouring a little hot blanc mange over eggs; blend; return to double boiler. Cook and stir 5 minutes longer. Pour into a mould or 6 dessert dishes. Cool. Garnish with whipped cream. Serves 6.

YOGURT

Heat until warm:

2 cups	**(500 mL)**	**milk**

For extra nutrition, mix in until dissolved:

2 tbsp.	**(30 mL)**	**noninstant skim milk powder (opt.)**

Stir in until blended:

1 tbsp.	**(15 mL)**	**fresh plain yogurt**

Warm a thermos bottle by rinsing it with boiling water, then pouring it out. Pour yogurt mixture into the warmed thermos. Cover tightly. Check after 3 hours for consistency; refrigerate as soon as yogurt has thickened. Will keep 5 days.

Serves 2.

FRUIT YOGURT

Add fruit to yogurt before refrigeration. Allow 2 hours to blend in flavours. Fruit may be sliced peaches, crushed pineapple, blueberries, strawberries, applesauce, sliced banana, etc.

FROZEN PINEAPPLE YOGURT

Stand container in hot water until dissolved:

1 tbsp.	**(15 mL)**	**gelatine**
4 tbsp.	**(60 mL)**	**unsweetened pineapple juice**

Stir in; chill until partially set; beat until light and frothy:

1½ cups	**(375 mL)**	**unsweetened pineapple juice**

Fold in:

1 cup	**(250 mL)**	**plain yogurt**
1 cup	**(250 mL)**	**well-drained crushed pineapple**

Freeze 2 to 2½ hours. It will freeze into a solid if left too long in freezer. Remove 20-30 minutes before serving to soften at room temperature.

Serves 6-8.

VARIATION:

FROZEN BANANA YOGURT: Replace crushed pineapple with sliced or mashed banana.

ORANGE SHERBET

Stand container in hot water until dissolved:

1 tbsp.	**(15 mL)**	**gelatine**
4 tbsp.	**(60 mL)**	**unsweetened concentrated orange juice, defrosted**

Stir into:

2⅔ cups	**(650 mL)**	**unsweetened orange juice**
2 tbsp.	**(30 mL)**	**lemon juice**

Freeze 2 to 2½ hours.

Serves 6.

STRAWBERRY MOUSSE

Stand container in hot water until dissolved:

1 tbsp.	**(15 mL)**	**gelatine**
6 tbsp.	**(90 mL)**	**unsweetened red grape juice**

Add:

2 cups	**(500 mL)**	**washed, hulled, crushed strawberries**
2 tbsp.	**(30 mL)**	**unsweetened concentrated pineapple juice, defrosted**
½ tsp.	**(2 mL)**	**vanilla OR strawberry extract**

Freeze until partially frozen. Beat until light and frothy.

Fold into:

1 cup	**(250 mL)**	**whipping cream, whipped**

Freeze 2 to 2½ hours. It will freeze into a solid if left too long in freezer. Remove 20 to 30 minutes before serving to soften at room temperature.

Serves 6-8.

VANILLA ICE CREAM

Beat with wire whisk in top part of double boiler until blended:

¾ cup	**(175 mL)**	**milk**
1 tbsp.	**(15 mL)**	**cornstarch**
1	**(1)**	**egg**

Beat into egg mixture:

½ cup	**(125 mL)**	**unsweetened concentrated mixed fruit juice, defrosted**

Cook and stir over hot (not boiling) water until mixture coats the spoon, 8 to 10 minutes. Cool.

Stir in and then chill at least 1 hour:

2 tsp.	**(10 mL)**	**vanilla**

Beat on low until thick, but not stiff:

2 cups	**(500 mL)**	**whipping cream**

Add chilled mixture, beating only until blended.

Freeze 2 to 2½ hours. It will freeze into a solid if left too long in freezer. Remove 20 to 30 minutes before serving to soften at room temperature.

Serves 8.

Fillings

CREAM FILLING

Beat in a saucepan until well blended:

3 tbsp.	**(45 mL)**	**cornstarch**
2	**(2)**	**egg yolks**
6 tbsp.	**(90 mL)**	**unsweetened concentrated apple juice, defrosted**

Add, cook and stir until thick:

1⅔ cups	**(400 mL)**	**hot milk**

Remove from heat. Add:

1 tsp.	**(5 mL)**	**vanilla**

Warm filling may be used in a pie shell but cool before spreading on cake. Will fill a 9" (23 cm) pie. Make half the recipe to fill a 9" (23 cm) layer cake.

ORANGE FILLING

Combine in a saucepan; cook and stir until thick:

2 tbsp.	**(30 mL)**	**cornstarch**
¾ cup	**(175 mL)**	**water**

Beat until well blended:

1	**(1)**	**egg, beaten**
6 tbsp.	**(90 mL)**	**unsweetened concentrated orange juice, defrosted**
¼ tsp.	**(1 mL)**	**grated orange rind**
½ tsp.	**(2 mL)**	**lemon juice**

Stir into starch mixture. Cook about 3 minutes. Cool before spreading on cake. Will fill an 8" (20 cm) layer cake.

VARIATION:

ORANGE-LEMON FILLING: Prepare Orange Filling, but add ¼ tsp. (1 mL) grated lemon rind. Increase lemon juice to 3 tbsp. (45 mL). Will fill a jelly roll.

CUSTARD FILLING

Combine in top part of double boiler until smooth:

3 tbsp. (45 mL) cornstarch
6 tbsp. (90 mL) milk

Mix in:

1½ cups (375 mL) milk, scalded

Cook and stir over boiling water until thick.

Beat just until blended:

2 (2) eggs
5 tbsp. (75 mL) unsweetened concentrated apple juice, defrosted

Add 2 tbsp. (30 mL) hot mixture; blend; return to double boiler. Cook and stir 5 minutes. Cool.

Stir in:

1 tsp. (5 mL) vanilla

Makes 2 cups (500 mL).

VARIATION:

CUSTARD CREAM FILLING: Fold cooled Custard Filling into ¾ cup (175 mL) whipping cream, whipped.

COTTAGE CHEESE FILLING

Blend in a blender until smooth:

2 cups (500 mL) cottage cheese
4 tbsp. (60 mL) unsweetened concentrated apple juice, defrosted
⅓ cup (75 mL) mashed ripe banana

Use as a filling for Cream Puffs, Eclairs, Blintzes, etc.

Makes 2½ cups (625 mL).

PINEAPPLE FILLING

Beat in a saucepan until blended:

1 tbsp.	**(15 mL)**	**cornstarch**
1	**(1)**	**egg yolk**
2 tbsp.	**(30 mL)**	**unsweetened concentrated pineapple juice, defrosted**

Add, cook and stir until thick:

½ cup	**(125 mL)**	**juice drained from crushed pineapple**

Remove from heat and add:

⅔ cup	**(150 mL)**	**well-drained unsweetened crushed pineapple**
½ tsp.	**(2 mL)**	**almond extract**

Will fill an 8" (20 cm) layer cake.

DATE FILLING

Bring to a boil, then reduce heat to low:

1 cup	**(250 mL)**	**chopped pitted dates**
1 cup	**(250 mL)**	**hot water**

Simmer and stir until thick and smooth. Remove from heat.

Add:

2 tsp.	**(10 mL)**	**unsweetened orange juice**

Will fill a 8" (20 cm) cake or date square.

FIG FILLING

Bring to a boil, then reduce heat to low:

15	**(15)**	**figs, stems removed, cut in small pieces**
1 cup	**(250 mL)**	**unsweetened orange juice**

Simmer and stir until thick and smooth. Remove from heat.

Will fill 27 fig bars.

APPLE FILLING

Cook and stir until soft, about 12 minutes:

3	**(3)**	**medium apples, peeled, grated**
3 tbsp.	**(45 mL)**	**unsweetened concentrated apple juice, defrosted**
¼ tsp.	**(1 mL)**	**grated lemon rind**
1 tbsp.	**(15 mL)**	**lemon juice**

Will fill an 8" (20 cm) round cake.

RAISIN FILLING

Combine in a saucepan until dissolved:

2 tbsp.	**(30 mL)**	**cornstarch**
¼ cup	**(50 mL)**	**unsweetened orange juice**
1 tsp.	**(5 mL)**	**lemon juice**

Add:

1¼ cups	**(300 mL)**	**unsweetened orange juice**
2 cups	**(500 mL)**	**raisins**

Cook and stir until thick.

Will fill a 9" (23 cm) pie.

INSTANT AND NONINSTANT SKIM MILK POWDER:

In food preparation, milk powder must be dissolved or beaten until smooth or the finished product would be gritty or stringy. Milk powder, especially the instant type, when added to flour, will affect the rising properties in baking. Avoid using more than 2 tbsp. (30 mL) to 1 cup (250 mL) of flour.

To prepare milk, measure into a measuring cup:
2 tbsp. (30 mL) noninstant skim milk powder OR
⅓ cup (75 mL) instant skim milk powder
Add water until it reaches the 1 cup (250 mL) mark.

TO TOAST COCONUT:

Spread coconut on a baking sheet in a 350°F (180°C) oven. Bake 2 minutes. Stir. Repeat 2 more times or until the desired colour has been reached.

Puddings

STEAMED CHRISTMAS PUDDING

Combine:

1¼ cups	**(300 mL)**	**toasted bread crumbs**
1 tsp.	**(5 mL)**	**grated orange rind**
½ tsp.	**(2 mL)**	**grated lemon rind**
¾ cup	**(175 mL)**	**wine OR unsweetened white grape juice**
½ cup	**(125 mL)**	**unsweetened concentrated mixed fruit juice, defrosted**

Sift together:

1¼ cups	**(300 mL)**	**sifted all-purpose flour**
1 tsp.	**(5 mL)**	**baking powder**
½ tsp.	**(2 mL)**	**baking soda**
1 tsp.	**(5 mL)**	**cinnamon**
½ tsp.	**(2 mL)**	**allspice**
¼ tsp.	**(1 mL)**	**nutmeg**

Add:

1½ cups	**(375 mL)**	**raisins**
¾ cup	**(175 mL)**	**currants**
1 cup	**(250 mL)**	**finely chopped figs**

Beat thoroughly:

3	**(3)**	**eggs**
2 tbsp.	**(30 mL)**	**vegetable oil**

Beat in bread crumb mixture. Stir in dry ingredients. Pour into a large, buttered or oiled mould or pudding dish. Cover with wax paper or foil and tie with string. Steam over boiling water 50 to 60 minutes or until a toothpick inserted in centre comes out clean. Serve with:

Rum Sauce, page 79

Serves 10.

STEAMED DATE AND WALNUT PUDDING

Combine and set aside until cooled:

½ cup	**(125 mL)**	**chopped pitted dates**
½ cup	**(125 mL)**	**boiling water**

Sift together:

1¼ cups	**(300 mL)**	**sifted all-purpose flour**
2 tsp.	**(10 mL)**	**baking powder**
½ tsp.	**(2 mL)**	**baking soda**
½ tsp.	**(2 mL)**	**cinnamon**

Add:

½ cup	**(125 mL)**	**chopped walnuts**

Beat thoroughly:

1	**(1)**	**egg**
4 tbsp.	**(60 mL)**	**unsweetened concentrated orange juice, defrosted**
2 tbsp.	**(30 mL)**	**vegetable oil**

Mix in cooled mixture. Add dry ingredients. Stir just enough to blend. Pour into an oiled 1½-quart (1.5 litre) mould and cover with lid or foil. Place on rack in steamer or large kettle. Add boiling water to ⅓ up sides of dish. Steam until done, 30 to 40 minutes. Cut in wedges while hot and serve with thin cream or any sweet sauce.

Serves 4-6.

STEAMED FRUIT AND WALNUT PUDDING

Add to date and boiling water mixture in the Steamed Date and Walnut recipe:

¼ cup	**(50 mL)**	**raisins**
½ tsp.	**(2 mL)**	**grated orange rind**
4	**(4)**	**apricots, finely chopped**
4	**(4)**	**figs, finely chopped**

Complete as for Steamed Date and Walnut Pudding.

CORNMEAL PUDDING

Cook and stir 20 minutes over boiling water in double boiler:

⅓ cup	**(75 mL)**	**cornmeal**
3 cups	**(750 mL)**	**milk**

Add, mix and pour into an oiled 1½-quart (1.5 litre) casserole:

4 tbsp.	**(60 mL)**	**unsweetened concentrated apple juice, defrosted**
½ tsp.	**(2 mL)**	**cinnamon**
¼ tsp.	**(1 mL)**	**ginger**

Bake 15 minutes at 300°F (150°C). Stir. Bake another 15 minutes.

Stir, then pour over top:

½ cup	**(125 mL)**	**cold milk**

Bake 1 hour. Shut off oven. Leave pudding in closed oven for another hour. Serve warm with thin cream or any sweet sauce.

Serves 4-6.

CARROT PUDDING

Sift together:

1¼ cups	**(300 mL)**	**sifted all-purpose flour**
1 tsp.	**(5 mL)**	**baking powder**
½ tsp.	**(2 mL)**	**baking soda**
½ tsp.	**(2 mL)**	**cinnamon**

Add:

½ cup	**(125 mL)**	**raisins**

Beat until blended:

1	**(1)**	**egg, beaten**
2 tbsp.	**(30 mL)**	**vegetable oil**
½ cup	**(125 mL)**	**unsweetened concentrated orange juice**
3 tbsp.	**(45 mL)**	**water**
1 tsp.	**(5 mL)**	**vanilla**
1 cup	**(250 mL)**	**grated raw carrots**

Add flour mixture. Stir just enough to blend. Pour into an oiled 8" (20 cm) diameter baking dish. Bake at 350°F (180°C) for 35 to 45 minutes or until a toothpick inserted in centre comes out clean. Serve warm with any sweet sauce.

Serves 6.

Apple-Cheese Crêpe Cake, page 73
Strawberry Sauce, page 80

FRUIT GRUNT

In a heavy saucepan with a lid, cook and stir until boiling:

2 cups	**(500 mL)**	**fruit (sliced apples, pears, blueberries, etc.)**
¾ cup	**(175 mL)**	**unsweetened concentrated fruit juice, defrosted**
¾ cup	**(175 mL)**	**water**

Turn off heat. Cover to keep mixture hot.

Sift together:

1 cup	**(250 mL)**	**sifted all-purpose flour**
1½ tsp.	**(7 mL)**	**baking powder**
¼ tsp.	**(1 mL)**	**baking soda**

Combine:

1 tbsp.	**(15 mL)**	**vegetable oil**
½ cup	**(125 mL)**	**unsweetened fruit juice**

Stir into flour mixture. Drop batter by spoonfuls on the hot mixture. Cover tightly. DO NOT PEEK. Cook over medium heat, 18 to 20 minutes. Serve hot.

Serves 6.

RICE PUDDING

Beat until blended:

2	**(2)**	**eggs, beaten**
½ cup	**(125 mL)**	**mashed ripe banana, mash with fork**
1¼ cups	**(300 mL)**	**milk**

Mix in:

1¼ cups	**(300 mL)**	**cooked rice**
⅓ cup	**(75 mL)**	**raisins**
½ cup	**(125 mL)**	**unsweetened concentrated mixed fruit juice, defrosted**
1 tsp.	**(5 mL)**	**vanilla**
½ tsp.	**(2 mL)**	**cinnamon (optional)**

Pour into a buttered or oiled 1½-quart (1.5 litre) baking dish. Bake at 325°F (160°C) until firm, 45 to 55 minutes. Serve with thin cream or Custard Sauce, page 76.

Serves 5-6.

ORANGE-LEMON SOUFFLÉ

Sift together:

5 tbsp.	**(75 mL)**	**all-purpose flour**
¼ tsp.	**(1 mL)**	**baking powder**
¼ tsp.	**(1 mL)**	**baking soda**

Beat until stiff and glossy:

3	**(3)**	**egg whites**

Beat until very thick:

3	**(3)**	**egg yolks**

Beat into egg yolks until blended, the flour mixture and:

1 tbsp.	**(15 mL)**	**lemon juice**
6 tbsp.	**(90 mL)**	**unsweetened concentrated orange juice, defrosted**
¼ tsp.	**(1 mL)**	**grated lemon rind**
¼ tsp.	**(1 mL)**	**grated orange rind**

Add to yolk mixture and beat well:

1½ cups	**(375 mL)**	**milk**

Fold in beaten egg whites. Pour into a 2-quart (2 L) baking dish. Oven poach by setting dish in a pan of hot water. Bake 50 to 60 minutes at 350°F (180°C). Serve immediately.

Serves 6.

ORANGE TAPIOCA PUDDING

Cook and stir over medium heat until boiling:

4 tbsp.	**(60 mL)**	**quick-cooking tapioca**
¼ tsp.	**(1 mL)**	**grated orange rind**
⅔ cup	**(150 mL)**	**unsweetened concentrated orange juice**
1½ cups	**(375 mL)**	**hot water**

Cook and stir I minute longer. Remove from heat.

Peel, separate segments and remove membrane from:

1	**(1)**	**orange**

Cut each segment into 3 pieces. Mix gently into pudding. Spoon into pedestal dessert glasses. Garnish with whipped cream.

If desired, fold cooled pudding into the whipped cream before spooning into dessert glasses.

Serves 5-6.

OLD-FASHIONED TAPIOCA PUDDING

Soak 5 hours in top part of double boiler:

⅓ cup	**(75 mL)**	**pearl tapioca**
1¾ cups	**(425 mL)**	**hot milk**

Cover and cook over boiling water for 30 minutes; stir occasionally. Turn heat off.

Stir in:

4 tbsp.	**(60 mL)**	**unsweetened concentrated fruit juice, defrosted**
⅓ cup	**(75 mL)**	**mashed ripe banana, mash with fork**
½ tsp.	**(2 mL)**	**vanilla**

Pour into individual serving dishes. Serve warm, or cooled, with thin cream or any sweet sauce.

Serves 4.

VARIATION:

SAGO PUDDING: Replace ⅓ cup (75 mL) pearl tapioca in the Old-Fashioned Tapioca Pudding recipe with same amount of sago. Reduce soaking time to 2½ hours and cooking time to 20 minutes.

Serves 4.

BREAD PUDDING

Combine in a buttered 1½-quart (1.5 L) baking dish:

3	**(3)**	**slices day-old bread, in ½" (1.3 cm) cubes**
1½ cups	**(375 mL)**	**milk**

Beat together:

2	**(2)**	**eggs, beaten**
½ cup	**(125 mL)**	**mashed ripe banana, mash with fork**
½ cup	**(125 mL)**	**unsweetened concentrated fruit juice**

Stir into bread mixture. Bake at 350°F (180°C) until well browned, 40 to 50 minutes. Serve hot or cooled with any sweet sauce.

Serves 6.

VARIATION:

RAISIN BREAD PUDDING: Add ½ cup (125 mL) raisins to Bread Pudding.

SELF-SAUCING APPLE PUDDING

Sift together:

1 cup	**(250 mL)**	**sifted all-purpose flour**
1½ tsp.	**(7 mL)**	**baking powder**
½ tsp.	**(2 mL)**	**baking soda**
½ tsp.	**(2 mL)**	**cinnamon**
½ tsp.	**(2 mL)**	**nutmeg**

Combine:

1 tbsp.	**(15 mL)**	**vegetable oil**
5 tbsp.	**(75 mL)**	**unsweetened concentrated apple juice, defrosted**
3 tbsp.	**(45 mL)**	**water**
⅔ cup	**(150 mL)**	**peeled, grated apples**

Stir in flour mixture. Spread in buttered or oiled 1½-quart (1.5 L) pudding dish.

Heat to boiling point:

2 cups	**(500 mL)**	**unsweetened apple juice**
½ cup	**(125 mL)**	**peeled, grated apples**

Pour over batter. DO NOT STIR! Bake at 350°F (180°C) until golden brown, about 35 minutes. Serve warm.

Serves 4-5.

VARIATION:

SELF-SAUCING PEACH PUDDING: Prepare Self-Saucing Apple Pudding, but omit the nutmeg. Replace grated apples with peeled, sliced peaches.

TO UNMOULD GELATINE DESSERTS:

Invert the dish of gelatine dessert onto a serving plate. Wear a pair of rubber gloves to wring out a dish towel soaked in very hot water. Wrap hot towel around dish and hold for a few minutes.

TO STEAM PUDDINGS:

Have water boiling at all times when steaming puddings. If water must be added, be sure it is boiling.

Pancakes and Crêpes

PLAIN PANCAKES

Sift together:

1 cup	**(250 mL)**	**sifted all-purpose flour**
2 tsp.	**(10 mL)**	**baking powder**

Beat until blended:

1	**(1)**	**egg**
2 tsp.	**(10 mL)**	**vegetable oil**
1 cup	**(250 mL)**	**milk**
1 tbsp.	**(15 mL)**	**unsweetened concentrated fruit juice**

Add to flour mixture. Beat until smooth. Drop by spoonfuls on hot, lightly oiled griddle. When full of bubbles, turn, brown other side. Serve hot.

Makes 12.

VARIATION:

SOUR MILK PANCAKES: Replace 2 tsp. (10 mL) baking powder in Plain Pancake recipe with ½ tsp. (2 mL) baking powder and ¾ tsp. (4 mL) baking soda; substitute the milk with same amount of sour milk.

WHOLE-WHEAT PANCAKES: Replace all-purpose flour in Plain Pancake recipe with whole-wheat flour. Stir whole-wheat flour, do not sift.

APPLE PANCAKES: Add to flour mixture in Plain Pancake recipe ½ tsp. (2 mL) cinnamon and ¾ cup (175 mL) peeled, grated apples.

BANANA PANCAKES: Beat with egg mixture in Plain Pancake recipe, ½ cup (125 mL) mashed ripe banana.

BLUEBERRY PANCAKES: Fold ½ cup (125 mL) blueberries into batter.

COTTAGE CHEESE PANCAKES

Sift together:

6 tbsp.	**(90 mL)**	**all-purpose flour**
1 tsp.	**(5 mL)**	**baking powder**

Beat until stiff:

2	**(2)**	**egg whites**

Beat until blended:

2	**(2)**	**egg yolks**
1 cup	**(250 mL)**	**cottage cheese**
½ cup	**(125 mL)**	**milk**
1 tbsp.	**(15 mL)**	**unsweetened concentrated fruit juice, defrosted**

Stir in flour mixture. Fold in egg whites. Drop from spoon onto hot oiled griddle. Brown both sides. Serve hot with applesauce, pureéd fruit or sour cream.

Serves 2-4.

BRAN PANCAKES

Sift together:

⅔ cup	**(150 mL)**	**sifted all-purpose flour**
1½ tsp.	**(7 mL)**	**baking powder**
½ tsp.	**(2 mL)**	**baking soda**

Beat until blended:

1	**(1)**	**egg**
1 tbsp.	**(15 mL)**	**vegetable oil**
¾ cup	**(175 mL)**	**milk**
2 tbsp.	**(30 mL)**	**unsweetened concentrated fruit juice, defrosted**

Mix in:

⅔ cup	**(150 mL)**	**natural bran**

Stir in flour mixture. Drop by spoonfuls onto hot, lightly oiled griddle. Turn. Brown other side.

Makes 12 (3½" or 9 cm).

CORNMEAL PANCAKES

Combine and set aside until cooled:

1 cup	**(250 mL)**	**milk, scalded**
½ cup	**(125 mL)**	**cornmeal**

Sift together:

⅔ cup	**(150 mL)**	**sifted all-purpose flour**
1 tsp.	**(5 mL)**	**baking powder**
¼ tsp.	**(1 mL)**	**baking soda**

Beat until blended:

1	**(1)**	**egg**
2 tsp.	**(10 mL)**	**vegetable oil**
6 tbsp.	**(90 mL)**	**unsweetened orange juice**

Mix in cooled mixture. Stir in flour mixture. Drop from spoon onto hot, lightly oiled griddle. Brown both sides.

Makes 12 small pancakes.

OATMEAL PANCAKES

Combine and set aside until cooled:

1 cup	**(250 mL)**	**milk, scalded**
1 cup	**(250 mL)**	**quick-cooking rolled oats**

Mix together:

¼ cup	**(50 mL)**	**all-purpose OR unbleached flour**
½ tsp.	**(2 mL)**	**baking powder**
¾ tsp.	**(4 mL)**	**baking soda**

Beat together:

1	**(1)**	**egg**
1 tbsp.	**(15 mL)**	**vegetable oil**
3 tbsp.	**(45 mL)**	**unsweetened fruit juice**

Stir in oats and milk. Add flour mixture. Drop from spoon onto hot, lightly oiled griddle. Brown both sides.

Makes 16, 3" (7.5 cm) pancakes.

TO MAKE MILK SOUR:

Place 1 tbsp. (15 mL) vinegar or lemon juice in a measuring cup. Pour in milk until it reaches the 1 cup (250 mL) mark.

SLICED APPLE PANCAKES

Sift together:

⅔ cup	**(150 mL)**	**sifted all-purpose flour**
1 tsp.	**(5 mL)**	**baking powder**
¼ tsp.	**(1 mL)**	**baking soda**
½ tsp.	**(2 mL)**	**cinnamon**

Beat until blended:

1	**(1)**	**egg**
2 tsp.	**(10 mL)**	**vegetable oil**
¾ cup	**(175 mL)**	**milk**
2 tbsp.	**(30 mL)**	**unsweetened concentrated apple juice, defrosted**

Stir in flour mixture. Let stand 15 minutes.

Peel, core and slice into 16 rings:

2	**(2)**	**medium apples**

Fry slices in buttered frying pan until cooked through, turning once.

Make small pancakes by pouring batter from tip of a spoon onto a hot lightly oiled griddle. Cook until set and brown. Place a slice of apple on each. Spoon a thin layer of batter to cover. Turn and brown other side. Serve at once with butter.

Makes 16.

CRÊPES

Blend until smooth:

2	**(2)**	**eggs**
1 tbsp.	**(15 mL)**	**vegetable oil**
1½ cups	**(375 mL)**	**milk**
1 cup	**(250 mL)**	**sifted all-purpose flour**

Cover and refrigerate at least 1 hour. Heat a 6" (15 cm) frying pan over medium heat. Lightly grease with a few drops of oil. Pour 2 to 3 tbsp. (30 to 45 mL) of batter all at once; rotate pan quickly to cover bottom. Lightly brown both sides.

Crêpes may be frozen for future use. Place wax paper between each for easy separation.

Makes 18.

APPLE-CHEESE CRÊPE CAKE

Prepare:

Cottage Cheese Filling, page 59
Crêpes, page 72

pour 5 tbsp. (75 mL) batter to cover a hot, lightly oiled 10" (25 cm) nonstick griddle. Make 4.

Wash, peel, cut into quarters and remove cores:

6 OR 7 (6 OR 7) cooking apples, depending on size

Cut each quarter into 3 wedges and place in a saucepan with:

6 tbsp. (90 mL) unsweetened concentrated apple juice, defrosted
1 tsp. (5 mL) cinnamon

Cook and stir carefully until apples are cooked through, 15 minutes.

Lay a crêpe in a baking dish. Arrange apples in circular pattern on top. Add another crêpe. Spread half of Cottage Cheese Filling evenly. Repeat with crêpe, apples, crêpe, ending with Cottage Cheese Filling. Bake at 325°F (160°C) just until heated through, about 15 minutes. Cut into wedges. Serve immediately. If desired, serve with:

Strawberry Sauce, page 80

Serves 6-8. See photograph page 64A.

USEFUL FACTS ABOUT PANCAKES AND CRÊPES:

Test pan for cooking pancakes or crêpes by sprinkling drops of cold water on it. If the drops spread out, the pan is not hot enough. If they immediately break up and evaporate, the temperature is too high. If they bounce and crackle, the pan is ready.

Keep pancakes or crêpes warm by placing them in a baking dish in a 200°F (100°C) oven. Separate them with wax paper and cover with a clean tea towel.

Store pancakes or crêpes with wax paper between each in plastic container. Place in refrigerator for up to 5 days, or in freezer for up to 6 weeks.

Reheat cold or frozen pancakes or crêpes by laying them overlapping in a lightly oiled, covered baking dish. Place in a 425°F (220°C) oven until heated through, 5 to 8 minutes.

BLINI (Russian Pancakes)

Scald and set aside until lukewarm:

2½ cups	**(625 mL)**	**milk**

Allow 5 minutes to dissolve:

1 tbsp.	**(15 mL)**	**granular yeast**
½ cup	**(125 mL)**	**warm water**

Add dissolved yeast to 1 cup (250 mL) lukewarm milk and stir in:

1 cup	**(250 mL)**	**buckwheat flour (first amount)**

Beat well, cover; set in warm place until bubbly, 2 to 2½ hours.

Beat together the bubbly mixture, the remaining milk and:

4	**(4)**	**egg yolks**
1 tbsp.	**(15 mL)**	**melted butter OR vegetable oil**
1 tbsp.	**(15 mL)**	**unsweetened concentrated apple juice, defrosted**

Add; mix well:

1 cup	**(250 mL)**	**buckwheat flour (second amount)**

Beat until stiff:

4	**(4)**	**egg whites**

Fold into batter. Cover and let rise 30 minutes. Make small pancakes on a hot, lightly oiled griddle. Brown both sides. Serve with melted butter, sour cream and caviar.

Serves 6-8.

TO SHELL EGGS EASILY:

Use eggs that are at least 2 weeks old for easy shelling. Fresh eggs cannot be shelled neatly.

Drain the water from the cooked eggs and shake the pot to crack the shells. Run cold water to cover eggs. The cold water will seep through the cracks on the eggs to make shelling easy.

STRAWBERRY CRÊPES SUZETTE

Stack 8 crêpes, page 72, with wax paper between each, in a baking dish. Keep warm in 200°F (100°C) oven.

Mix well:

8 oz.	**(240 g)**	**sliced strawberries**
4 tbsp.	**(60 mL)**	**unsweetened concentrated orange juice, defrosted**

Combine:

		grated rind of ½ an orange
		grated rind of ½ a lemon
6 tbsp.	**(90 mL)**	**unsweetened concentrated orange juice, defrosted**
½ cup	**(125 mL)**	**sherry**
½ cup	**(125 mL)**	**water**

Roll 1 oz. (30 g) sliced berries in each crêpe.

Melt in a chafing dish:

3 tbsp.	**(45 mL)**	**butter**

Stir in sherry mixture and the juice from the berries. Heat until bubbling. Add crêpes, spooning sauce over each.

Drizzle over crêpes:

½ cup	**(125 mL)**	**brandy**

Ignite. Spoon flaming sauce over crêpes. Serve as soon as flame dies.

Serves 4.

TO DIFFERENTIATE COOKED FROM RAW EGGS IN SHELL:

Cooked eggs will spin round and round. Raw eggs will not spin, but sway from side to side.

Sweet Sauces and Syrups

CUSTARD SAUCE

Beat with a wire whisk in a saucepan until blended:

1	**(1)**	**egg**
1 tbsp.	**(15 mL)**	**cornstarch**
4 tbsp.	**(60 mL)**	**unsweetened concentrated apple juice, defrosted**

Add:

1½ cups	**(375 mL)**	**milk**

Cook and stir until thick. Remove from heat.

Beat in:

½ tsp.	**(2 mL)**	**vanilla**

Serves 6-8.

APRICOT SAUCE

Bring to a boil; reduce heat to medium-low:

10	**(10)**	**dried apricots**
½ cup	**(125 mL)**	**unsweetened orange juice**

Cook and stir until all juice has evaporated.

Add:

1 cup	**(250 mL)**	**unsweetened orange juice**
1 tsp.	**(5 mL)**	**almond extract**

Blend until smooth.

Serves 6.

FOAMY SAUCE

Combine in a saucepan:

2 tbsp.	**(30 mL)**	**melted butter**
2 tbsp.	**(30 mL)**	**flour**

Beat thoroughly:

1	**(1)**	**egg yolk**
⅔ cup	**(150 mL)**	**unsweetened concentrated fruit juice, defrosted**
⅔ cup	**(150 mL)**	**water**

Add to butter mixture. Stir and cook until thick.

Just before serving, beat until stiff:

1	**(1)**	**egg white**

Fold into sauce.

Serves 6.

BLUEBERRY SAUCE

Combine in a saucepan:

1 tbsp.	**(15 mL)**	**cornstarch**
½ tsp.	**(2 mL)**	**cinnamon**
½ cup	**(125 mL)**	**unsweetened concentrated orange juice, defrosted**

Add; stir and cook over medium heat until clear and smooth:

¾ cup	**(175 mL)**	**water**

Mix in:

⅔ cup	**(150 mL)**	**fresh blueberries**

Cook and stir 1 minute longer. Serve hot.

Serves 6.

LEMON SAUCE

Combine in a saucepan:

1 tbsp.	**(15 mL)**	**cornstarch**
1 tsp.	**(5 mL)**	**grated lemon rind**
1 tbsp.	**(15 mL)**	**unsweetened concentrated apple juice, defrosted**
3 tbsp.	**(45 mL)**	**lemon juice**

Add; stir and cook over medium heat until clear and smooth:

2 tsp.	**(10 mL)**	**butter**
1 cup	**(250 mL)**	**unsweetened pineapple juice**

Serve hot on puddings, plain cakes or sponge cakes.

Serves 6.

ORANGE SAUCE

Combine in a saucepan:

4 tsp.	**(20 mL)**	**cornstarch**
¼ tsp.	**(1 mL)**	**grated orange rind**
6 tbsp.	**(90 mL)**	**unsweetened concentrated orange juice**

Add; stir and cook over medium heat until clear and smooth:

1 cup	**(250 mL)**	**water**

Serve hot.

Serves 6.

VARIATIONS:

CHUNKY ORANGE SAUCE: Peel 1 orange, separate segments, remove membrane. Cut each segment into 3 pieces. Add to Orange Sauce.

ORANGE-RAISIN SAUCE: Add ¼ cup (50 mL) raisins to Orange OR Chunky Orange Sauce recipe.

ORANGE-LEMON SAUCE: Add to Orange Sauce recipe 1 tbsp. (15 mL) lemon juice and ¼ tsp. (1 mL) grated lemon rind.

FRUIT-JUICE SAUCE: In the Orange Sauce recipe, replace the grated orange rind and the unsweetened concentrated orange juice with 5 tbsp. (75 mL) unsweetened concentrated mixed fruit juice.

FRUIT SAUCE: Add ⅓ cup (75 mL) diced fruit to Fruit-Juice Sauce.

RUM SAUCE

Combine in a saucepan:

5 tsp.	**(25 mL)**	**cornstarch**
2 tbsp.	**(30 mL)**	**unsweetened concentrated fruit juice, defrosted**

Add; stir and cook over medium heat until clear and smooth:

1¼ cups	**(300 mL)**	**unsweetened white grape juice**

Mix in:

2 tsp.	**(10 mL)**	**butter**
2 tbsp.	**(30 mL)**	**rum OR**
1 tsp.	**(5 mL)**	**rum flavouring**

Serve hot on Christmas Pudding, page 62, or any pudding.

Serves 6.

BRANDY SAUCE

Combine in a saucepan:

4 tsp.	**(20 mL)**	**cornstarch**
2 tbsp.	**(30 mL)**	**unsweetened concentrated pineapple juice, defrosted**

Add; stir and cook over medium heat until clear and smooth:

1 tbsp.	**(15 mL)**	**butter**
1 cup	**(250 mL)**	**unsweetened apple juice**

Just before serving, stir in:

3 tbsp.	**(45 mL)**	**brandy OR**
1¼ tsp.	**(6 mL)**	**brandy flavouring**

Serve hot on puddings, roast duck or baked ham.

Serves 6.

RASPBERRY SAUCE

Crush in a saucepan; if desired, strain to remove seeds:

10 oz.	**(284 g)**	**frozen raspberries, thawed**

Combine and add to berries:

2 tsp.	**(10 mL)**	**cornstarch**
2 tbsp.	**(30 mL)**	**unsweetened concentrated pineapple juice, defrosted**
2 tbsp.	**(30 mL)**	**water**

Cook and stir over medium-low heat until clear and smooth. Have sauce at room temperature to serve on fruit. Serve hot on pancakes.

Serves 4.

STRAWBERRY SAUCE

Crush:

1 cup	**(250 mL)**	**sliced fresh strawberries**

Combine in a saucepan:

1 tbsp.	**(15 mL)**	**cornstarch**
4 tbsp.	**(60 mL)**	**unsweetened red grape juice**

Mix in:

¾ cup	**(175 mL)**	**unsweetened red grape juice**

Cook and stir until thick and smooth. Add crushed berries. Serve hot on pancakes and cold on ice cream.

Serves 6. See photograph page 64A.

COTTAGE CHEESE DRESSING

Blend until smooth:

½ cup	**(125 mL)**	**cottage cheese**
3 tbsp.	**(45 mL)**	**unsweetened pineapple OR apple juice**

Serve over fruit or puddings.

Serves 4.

Carrot Cake, page 24
Apple Muffins, page 84
Blueberry Muffins, page 84
Cheese Muffins, page 84
Pineapple Jam, page 98
Apricot Jam, page 96
Lemon Butter, page 93
Cream Cheese Frosting, page 33

PINEAPPLE SYRUP

Blend until smooth:

¾ cup	**(175 mL)**	**undrained crushed pineapple**
½ cup	**(125 mL)**	**unsweetened pineapple juice**

Mix in saucepan until dissolved:

2 tsp.	**(10 mL)**	**cornstarch**
2 tbsp.	**(30 mL)**	**unsweetened concentrated pineapple juice, defrosted**

Add blended pineapple. Bring to a boil, then simmer and stir 2 minutes.

Serves 6.

FIG SYRUP

Bring to a boil, then simmer and stir 5 minutes:

4	**(4)**	**figs, stems removed, sliced**
¾ cup	**(175 mL)**	**unsweetened orange juice**

Add:

⅓ cup	**(75 mL)**	**unsweetened orange juice**

Blend until smooth.

Serves 4-6.

RAISIN SYRUP

Blend until smooth:

½ cup	**(125 mL)**	**raisins**
¾ cup	**(175 mL)**	**unsweetened fruit juice**

Combine in a saucepan:

1 tsp.	**(5 mL)**	**cornstarch**
4 tbsp.	**(60 mL)**	**unsweetened fruit juice**

Add blended raisins. Bring to a boil, then simmer and stir 2 minutes longer.

Serves 4-6.

APPLE SYRUP (using applesauce)

Combine in a saucepan:

1 cup	**(250 mL)**	**applesauce**
4 tbsp.	**(60 mL)**	**unsweetened concentrated apple juice, defrosted**
½ cup	**(125 mL)**	**water**
¼ tsp.	**(1 mL)**	**cinnamon**
¼ tsp.	**(1 mL)**	**nutmeg**

Bring to a boil, then simmer and stir 2 minutes longer.

Serves 6-8.

APPLE SYRUP (using apple juice)

Combine in a saucepan:

1 tbsp.	**(15 mL)**	**cornstarch**
¼ tsp.	**(1 mL)**	**cinnamon**
¼ tsp.	**(1 mL)**	**nutmeg**
4 tbsp.	**(60 mL)**	**unsweetened apple juice**

Add:

1 cup	**(250 mL)**	**unsweetened apple juice**

Bring to a boil, then simmer and stir 2 minutes longer.

Serves 6.

Muffins, Quick Breads, Popovers and Scones

PLAIN MUFFINS

Sift together:

2 cups	**(500 mL)**	**sifted all-purpose flour**
3 tsp.	**(15 mL)**	**baking powder**
¼ tsp.	**(1 mL)**	**baking soda**

Beat until blended:

1	**(1)**	**large egg, beaten**
2 tbsp.	**(30 mL)**	**vegetable oil**
1 cup	**(250 mL)**	**milk**
2 tbsp.	**(30 mL)**	**unsweetened concentrated apple juice, defrosted**

Add to dry ingredients. Stir just enough to moisten flour. Fill oiled muffin cups ⅔ full. Bake at 400°F (200°C) until brown, about 20 minutes. Serve warm with butter or margarine and jam or marmalade.

Makes 12.

TO MAKE TENDER MUFFINS:

Too much stirring and beating makes muffins tough and coarse textured. Stir just enough to dampen flour.

SOUR MILK MUFFINS

Sift together:

2 cups	**(500 mL)**	**sifted all-purpose flour**
2 tsp.	**(10 mL)**	**baking powder**
½ tsp.	**(2 mL)**	**baking soda**

Beat until blended:

1	**(1)**	**large egg, beaten**
2 tbsp.	**(30 mL)**	**vegetable oil**
⅔ cup	**(150 mL)**	**sour milk**
½ cup	**(125 mL)**	**unsweetened fruit juice**

Add to dry ingredients.

Complete as for Plain Muffins.

VARIATIONS:

APPLE MUFFINS: Add to egg mixture in the Plain or Sour Milk Muffins 1 cup (250 mL) peeled grated apples. See photograph page 80A.

BLUEBERRY MUFFINS: Add to flour mixture in the Plain or Sour Milk Muffins, page 83, 84, 1 cup (250 mL) blueberries. See photograph page 80A.

CARROT MUFFINS: Add to egg mixture in the Plain or Sour Milk Muffins, page 83, 84, 1 cup (250 mL) grated carrots.

CHEESE MUFFINS: Add to flour mixture in the Plain or Sour Milk Muffins, page 83, 84, ½ cup (125 mL) grated cheese, 1 tsp. (5 mL) dry mustard, and a pinch of cayenne. See photograph page 80A.

100% WHOLE-WHEAT MUFFINS: Replace 2 cups (500 mL) all-purpose flour in the Plain or Sour Milk Muffins, page 83, 84, with same amount of whole-wheat flour, not sifted. If desired, add ½ cup (125 mL) raisins to the flour mixture.

FILLED MUFFINS: Fill muffin cups ¼ full of Plain or Sour Milk Muffin batter, page 83, 84. Mix together 2 tbsp. (30 mL) finely chopped nuts and 2 tbsp. (30 mL) jam, then spoon 1 tsp. (5 mL) nut mixture in centre of batter. Cover with more batter. Bake at 400°F (200°C) until brown, about 20 minutes. Makes 12.

PINEAPPLE MUFFINS

Sift together:

2 cups	**(500 mL)**	**sifted all-purpose flour**
3 tsp.	**(15 mL)**	**baking powder**
½ tsp.	**(2 mL)**	**baking soda**

Beat until well blended:

1	**(1)**	**large egg, beaten**
2 tbsp.	**(30 mL)**	**instant skim milk powder OR**
2 tsp.	**(10 mL)**	**noninstant skim milk powder**
2 tbsp.	**(30 mL)**	**vegetable oil**
2 tbsp.	**(30 mL)**	**unsweetened concentrated fruit juice, defrosted**
14 oz.	**(398 mL)**	**canned crushed pineapple, drain off**
4 tbsp.	**(60 mL)**	**of the pineapple juice**

Add dry ingredients. Stir just enough to moisten flour. Fill oiled muffin cups ⅔ full. Bake at 400°F (200°C) for 20 minutes or until brown.

Makes 12.

DATE MUFFINS

Bring to a boil, then simmer and stir until thick; cool:

1 cup	**(250 mL)**	**chopped pitted dates**
1¼ cups	**(300 mL)**	**unsweetened orange juice**

Sift together:

2 cups	**(500 mL)**	**sifted all-purpose flour**
2 tsp.	**(10 mL)**	**baking powder**
¾ tsp.	**(4 mL)**	**baking soda**

Beat until well blended:

1	**(1)**	**large egg, beaten**
2 tbsp.	**(30 mL)**	**instant skim milk powder OR**
2 tsp.	**(10 mL)**	**noninstant skim milk powder**
2 tbsp.	**(30 mL)**	**vegetable oil**

Blend in date mixture. Add dry ingredients. Stir just enough to moisten flour. Fill oiled muffin cups ⅔ full. Bake at 400°F (200°C) until brown, about 20 minutes.

Makes 12.

CORNMEAL MUFFINS

Combine and set aside until cooled:

1¼ cups	**(300 mL)**	**milk, scalded**
¾ cup	**(175 mL)**	**cornmeal**

Sift together:

1 cup	**(250 mL)**	**sifted all-purpose flour**
3 tsp.	**(15 mL)**	**baking powder**
½ tsp.	**(2 mL)**	**baking soda**

Beat until blended:

1	**(1)**	**large egg, beaten**
2 tbsp.	**(30 mL)**	**vegetable oil**
6 tbsp.	**(90 mL)**	**unsweetened concentrated apple juice, defrosted**

Stir in cooled mixture. Add dry ingredients. Stir just enough to moisten flour. Fill oiled muffin cups ⅔ full. Bake at 400°F (200°C) until brown, about 20 minutes.

Makes 12.

FIG OATMEAL MUFFINS

Combine and set aside until cooled:

¾ cup	**(175 mL)**	**milk, scalded**
1 cup	**(250 mL)**	**quick-cooking rolled oats**
6	**(6)**	**figs, finely chopped**

Complete as for Cornmeal Muffins.

Makes 12.

LEMON BREAD

Sift together:

2 cups	**(500 mL)**	**sifted all-purpose flour**
2 tsp.	**(10 mL)**	**baking powder**
1 tsp.	**(5 mL)**	**baking soda**

Cut in with pastry blender until mixture resembles fine crumbs:

5 tbsp.	**(75 mL)**	**butter OR margarine**

LEMON BREAD (continued)

Beat together:

1	**(1)**	**egg, beaten**
2 tbsp.	**(30 mL)**	**milk OR sour milk**
5 tbsp.	**(75 mL)**	**lemon juice**
5 tbsp.	**(75 mL)**	**unsweetened concentrated orange juice**
4 tbsp.	**(60 mL)**	**unsweetened concentrated apple juice**
1 tbsp.	**(15 mL)**	**grated lemon rind**

Add to flour mixture; stir just enough to blend. Pour into an 8 ½" X 4½" (22 cm X 11 cm) oiled, wax-paper-lined loaf pan. Allow to stand 20 minutes. Bake at 350°F (180°C) 50 to 60 minutes or until toothpick inserted in centre comes out clean. Cool 10 minutes on wire rack. Unmould.

For Lemon-Walnut Bread, add ¼ cup (50 mL) chopped walnuts to flour.

Makes 1 loaf.

CHEESE BREAD

Sift together:

2½ cups	**(625 mL)**	**sifted all-purpose flour**
2½ tsp.	**(12 mL)**	**baking powder**
¾ tsp.	**(4 mL)**	**baking soda**
1¼ tsp.	**(6 mL)**	**dry mustard**
¼ tsp.	**(1 mL)**	**paprika**
⅛ tsp.	**(0.5 mL)**	**cayenne**

Add:

1 cup	**(250 mL)**	**grated cheese**

Beat together:

1	**(1)**	**large egg, beaten**
3 tbsp.	**(45 mL)**	**vegetable oil**
1 cup	**(250 mL)**	**sour milk**
½ cup	**(125 mL)**	**unsweetened orange juice**

Add flour mixture; stir just enough to blend. Pour into a lightly oiled 9" X 5" (23 cm X 12.5 cm) nonstick loaf pan. Allow to stand 20 minutes. Bake at 350°F (180°C) for 50 to 60 minutes or until toothpick inserted in centre comes out clean. Cool 10 minutes on wire rack. Unmould. Brush top with melted butter or margarine.

Makes 1 loaf.

RAISIN-BRAN MUFFINS

Mix together:

1 cup	**(250 mL)**	**all-purpose OR unbleached flour**
3 tsp.	**(15 mL)**	**baking powder**
½ tsp.	**(2 mL)**	**baking soda**

Add:

1⅓ cups	**(325 mL)**	**natural bran**
⅔ cup	**(150 mL)**	**raisins**

Beat until blended:

1	**(1)**	**large egg, beaten**
2 tbsp.	**(30 mL)**	**vegetable oil**
¾ cup	**(175 mL)**	**milk**
4 tbsp.	**(60 mL)**	**unsweetened concentrated orange juice, defrosted**

Add dry ingredients. Stir just enough to moisten flour. Fill oiled muffin cups ⅔ full. Bake at 400°F (200°C) 20 minutes or until brown.

Makes 12.

WHEAT-GERM MUFFINS

Mix together:

1¼ cups	**(300 mL)**	**all-purpose OR unbleached flour**
2 tsp.	**(10 mL)**	**baking powder**
¾ tsp.	**(4 mL)**	**baking soda**

Add:

1 cup	**(250 mL)**	**wheat germ, preferably raw**
¼ cup	**(50 mL)**	**finely chopped nuts**

Beat until well blended:

1	**(1)**	**large egg, beaten**
2 tbsp.	**(30 mL)**	**instant skim milk powder OR**
2 tsp.	**(10 mL)**	**noninstant skim milk powder**
2 tbsp.	**(30 mL)**	**vegetable oil**
1 cup	**(250 mL)**	**unsweetened fruit juice**

Add dry ingredients. Stir just enough to moisten flour. Fill oiled muffin cups ⅔ full. Bake at 400°F (200°C) until brown, about 20 minutes.

Makes 12.

BANANA BRAN BREAD

Mix together:

1 cup	**(250 mL)**	**all-purpose flour OR unbleached flour**
2 tsp.	**(10 mL)**	**baking powder**
½ tsp.	**(2 mL)**	**baking soda**
½ tsp.	**(2 mL)**	**cinnamon**

Add:

½ cup	**(125 mL)**	**whole-wheat flour**
½ cup	**(125 mL)**	**natural bran**
½ cup	**(125 mL)**	**finely chopped pecans OR walnuts**

Beat together:

1	**(1)**	**large egg, beaten**
4 tbsp.	**(60 mL)**	**vegetable oil**
5 tbsp.	**(75 mL)**	**unsweetened orange juice**
3	**(3)**	**medium, ripe bananas, mash with fork**

Add flour mixture; stir to blend. Complete as Date Bran Bread, below.

Makes 1 loaf.

DATE-BRAN BREAD

Heat to boiling point; set aside until cooled:

1¼ cups	**(300 mL)**	**unsweetened orange juice**
¾ cups	**(175 mL)**	**finely chopped pitted dates**

Mix together:

2 cups	**(500 mL)**	**all-purpose OR unbleached flour**
2½ tsp.	**(12 mL)**	**baking powder**
½ tsp.	**(2 mL)**	**baking soda**

Beat until blended:

1	**(1)**	**large egg, beaten**
2 tbsp.	**(30 mL)**	**vegetable oil**
⅔ cup	**(150 mL)**	**natural bran**

Beat in dates and juice. Add flour mixture. Stir just enough to blend. Pour into a lightly oiled 9" X 5" (23 cm X 12.5 cm) nonstick loaf pan. Allow to stand 20 minutes. Bake at 350°F (180°C) for 50 to 60 minutes or until toothpick inserted in centre comes out clean. Cool 10 minutes on wire rack. Unmold.

Makes 1 loaf.

WHEAT-GERM BREAD

Mix together:

¾ cup	**(175 mL)**	**all-purpose OR unbleached flour**
2½ tsp.	**(12 mL)**	**baking powder**
½ tsp.	**(2 mL)**	**baking soda**

Add:

¾ cup	**(175 mL)**	**whole-wheat flour**
1¼ cups	**(300 mL)**	**wheat germ, preferably raw**
¼ cup	**(50 mL)**	**chopped nuts**
½ cup	**(125 mL)**	**raisins**

Beat until well blended:

1	**(1)**	**large egg, beaten**
2 tbsp.	**(30 mL)**	**instant skim milk powder OR**
2 tsp.	**(10 mL)**	**noninstant skim milk powder**
2 tbsp.	**(30 mL)**	**vegetable oil**
1¼ cups	**(300 mL)**	**unsweetened fruit juice**

Add flour mixture. Complete as for Date Bran Bread, page 89.

ZUCCHINI BREAD

Mix together:

1 cup	**(250 mL)**	**all-purpose OR unbleached flour**
2 tsp.	**(10 mL)**	**baking powder**
½ tsp.	**(2 mL)**	**baking soda**
1 tsp.	**(5 mL)**	**cinnamon**

Add:

1 cup	**(250 mL)**	**whole-wheat flour**
½ cup	**(125 mL)**	**raisins**

Beat together:

2	**(2)**	**egg, beaten**
2 tbsp.	**(30 mL)**	**vegetable oil**
6 tbsp.	**(90 mL)**	**unsweetened concentrated orange juice**
2 tbsp.	**(30 mL)**	**water**
1½ cups	**(375 mL)**	**coarsely grated zucchini**

Add flour mixture; stir just enough to blend. Pour into a lightly oiled 9" X 5" (23 cm X 12.5 cm) nonstick loaf pan. Allow to stand 20 minutes Bake at 350°F (180°C) for 50 to 55 minutes or until a toothpick inserted in centre comes out clean. Cool 10 minutes on wire rack. Unmould.

Makes 1 loaf.

POPOVERS

Beat until well blended:

2	**(2)**	**eggs**
1 cup	**(250 mL)**	**milk**
1 tbsp.	**(15 mL)**	**vegetable oil**

Beat in until smooth:

1 cup	**(250 mL)**	**sifted all-purpose flour**

Fill greased popover, muffin or custard cups half full. Bake at 425°F (220°C) for 20 minutes; reduce to 325°F (160°C) and bake 20 minutes longer. Serve at once.

Fill popovers for dessert with:

sliced fruit, whipped cream, jelly, etc.

Fill popovers for breakfast with:

scrambled eggs

Fill popovers for luncheon with:

creamed chicken, creamed fish, etc.

Makes 8.

OATMEAL POPOVERS

Beat until well blended:

2	**(2)**	**eggs**
1⅔ cups	**(400 mL)**	**milk**

Add and beat until smooth:

½ cup	**(125 mL)**	**quick-cooking rolled oats**
1 cup	**(250 mL)**	**sifted all-purpose flour**

Fill greased popover, muffin or custard cups half full. Bake at 425°F (220°C) 20 minutes; reduce to 325°F (160°C) and bake 20 minutes longer. Serve at once.

Makes 14-16.

TO PREVENT SOGGY POPOVERS:

Five minutes before popovers have finished baking, puncture them with a sharp fork to allow steam to escape.

SCONES

Sift together:

2 cups	**(500 mL)**	**sifted all-purpose flour**
3 tsp.	**(15 mL)**	**baking powder**
½ tsp.	**(2 mL)**	**baking soda**

Cut in coarsely with pastry blender:

4 tbsp.	**(60 mL)**	**shortening OR margarine**

Beat well:

1	**(1)**	**egg, beaten**
1 tbsp.	**(15 mL)**	**unsweetened concentrated apple juice, defrosted**
4 tbsp.	**(60 mL)**	**sour milk**

Add to flour mixture. Stir to make a soft dough. Knead 15 to 20 times on lightly floured board. Divide dough into half. Shape into 2 balls. Roll each ball into a round ½" to ¾" (1.5 cm) thickness. Transfer to a lightly oiled baking sheet. Cut each into 6 pie-shaped wedges. Do not separate. Brush tops with milk. Bake 12 to 15 minutes at 450°F (230°C). Serve hot with butter or margarine and jam or marmalade.

Makes 12.

TO FRESHEN STALE BREAD OR BUNS:

Place slices of bread or buns in a covered casserole. Steam over boiling water until soft, about 5 minutes.

Butters, Jams and Spreads

WHIPPED BUTTER OR MARGARINE

Whip until blended:

4 tbsp.	(60 mL)	**butter OR margarine, room temp.**
2 tsp.	(10 mL)	**milk**

Serves 4-6

LEMON BUTTER OR MARGARINE

Whip until blended:

4 tbsp.	(60 mL)	**butter OR margarine, room temp.**
2 tsp.	(10 mL)	**lemon juice**
¼ tsp.	(1 mL)	**grated lemon rind**

Serves 4-6. See photograph page 80A.

ORANGE BUTTER OR MARGARINE

Whip until blended:

4 tbsp.	(60 mL)	**butter OR margarine, room temp.**
2 tsp.	(10 mL)	**unsweetened orange juice**
¼ tsp.	(1 mL)	**grated orange rind**

Serves 4-6.

PARSLEY BUTTER OR MARGARINE

Whip until blended:

4 tbsp.	**(60 mL)**	**butter OR margarine, room temp.**
1 tbsp.	**(15 mL)**	**finely chopped parsley**
2 tsp.	**(10 mL)**	**lemon juice**
pinch	**(pinch)**	**white pepper**

Serves 4-6.

GARLIC BUTTER OR MARGARINE

Whip until blended:

4 tbsp.	**(60 mL)**	**butter OR margarine, room temp.**
2 tsp.	**(10 mL)**	**milk**
¼ tsp.	**(1 mL)**	**garlic powder OR**
1	**(1)**	**garlic clove, minced**

Serves 4-6.

PEANUT BUTTER

Blend in blender until desired smoothness:

1½ cups	**(375 mL)**	**roasted peanuts, unsalted**
3 tsp.	**(15 mL)**	**peanut oil (optional)**

Makes ¾ cup (175 mL).

GRAPE-JELLY SPREAD

Combine in a saucepan for 2 minutes to soften:

1½ tsp.	**(7 mL)**	**gelatine**
2 tbsp.	**(30 mL)**	**unsweetened concentrated apple juice, defrosted**

Add, stir and cook until mixture boils:

1 cup	**(250 mL)**	**unsweetened grape juice**

Mix in:

2 tsp.	**(10 mL)**	**lemon juice**

Makes 1 cup (250 mL).

APPLE BUTTER

Cook and stir until liquid has evaporated, about 15 minutes:

4	**(4)**	**medium apples, peeled, cored, sliced**
¼ cup	**(50 mL)**	**unsweetened apple juice**

Mash apples and add:

2 tbsp.	**(30 mL)**	**lemon juice**
2 tbsp.	**(30 mL)**	**vinegar**
¼ tsp.	**(1 mL)**	**grated lemon rind**
½ tsp.	**(2 mL)**	**cinnamon**
½ tsp.	**(2 mL)**	**nutmeg**
pinch	**(pinch)**	**cloves**

Cook and stir 2 minutes longer.

Makes 1¾ cups (425 mL).

CREAM CHEESE SPREAD

Beat until blended:

4.4 oz.	**(125 g)**	**cream cheese**
¼ cup	**(50 mL)**	**well-drained, crushed, canned OR stewed fruit**
4 tsp.	**(20 mL)**	**unsweetened concentrated apple juice, defrosted**

Makes ¾ cup (175 mL).

COTTAGE CHEESE SPREAD

Blend until smooth:

½ cup	**(125 mL)**	**cottage cheese**
4 tbsp.	**(60 mL)**	**jam of your choice, page 96 to 99**
4 tsp.	**(20 mL)**	**unsweetened concentrated apple juice, defrosted**

Makes ¾ cup (175 mL).

STRAWBERRY JAM I

Combine in a small saucepan for 2 minutes:

1½ tsp.	**(7 mL)**	**gelatine**
4 tbsp.	**(60 mL)**	**unsweetened concentrated pineapple juice**

Add:

1 tsp.	**(5 mL)**	**lemon juice**
1 cup	**(250 mL)**	**crushed fresh OR frozen strawberries**

Heat to boiling point, then reduce to medium-low. Cook and stir 1 minute longer.

Makes about 1 cup (250 mL).

VARIATION:

STRAWBERRY JAM II: Replace the 1½ tsp. (7 mL) gelatine in the Strawberry Jam I recipe with 4 tsp. (20 mL) cornstarch.

FRESH PLUM JAM

Blend in blender until almost smooth:

1½ cups	**(375 mL)**	**washed, pitted, chopped, fresh prune plums**
6 tbsp.	**(90 mL)**	**unsweetened concentrated orange juice**

Bring to a boil, then reduce heat to medium-low. Cook and stir 5 minutes or until desired thickness.

Stir in:

½ tsp.	**(2 mL)**	**cinnamon**
pinch	**(pinch)**	**cloves**

Makes about 1 cup (250 mL).

APRICOT JAM

Bring to a boil, then reduce to medium:

¾ cup	**(175 mL)**	**finely chopped dried apricots**
1½ cups	**(375 mL)**	**unsweetened orange juice**

Cook and stir 15 to 20 minutes or until desired thickness.

Makes about 1¼ cups (300 mL). See photograph page 80A.

DATE JAM

Bring to a boil, then reduce to low:

1½ cups	**(375 mL)**	**chopped pitted dates**
1 cup	**(250 mL)**	**water**
		grated rind of ½ an orange

Cook and stir until thick and smooth.

Makes about 1¼ cups (300 mL).

FIG JAM

Cut in very fine slices:

9	**(9)**	**figs, stems removed**

Place in a small saucepan with:

3 tbsp.	**(45 mL)**	**unsweetened concentrated orange juice, defrosted**
½ cup	**(125 mL)**	**water**

Cook and stir until mixture is thick.

Makes about 1 cup (250 mL).

PRUNE JAM

Soak 2 hours or overnight:

1 cup	**(250 mL)**	**finely chopped pitted prunes**
6 tbsp.	**(90 mL)**	**unsweetened concentrated orange juice, defrosted**
⅔ cup	**(150 mL)**	**water**
¼ tsp.	**(1 mL)**	**cinnamon**

Bring to a boil, then simmer and stir about 3 minutes, or until desired thickness.

Makes about 1¼ cups (300 mL).

FRUIT JAM

Cut in very fine slices:

4	**(4)**	**figs, stems removed**
9	**(9)**	**pitted prunes**
9	**(9)**	**dried apricots**

Soak 2 hours or overnight with:

1½ cups	**(375 mL)**	**unsweetened fruit juice**

Bring to a boil, then reduce heat to low. Cook and stir 3 minutes or until desired thickness.

Makes about 2 cups (500 mL).

PEAR JAM

Bring to a boil, then reduce to medium-low:

2	**(2)**	**pears, washed, cored, crushed**
4 tbsp.	**(60 mL)**	**unsweetened concentrated apple juice, defrosted**
1 tsp.	**(5 mL)**	**minced ginger root**
		grated rind of ½ a lemon

Cook and stir 3 minutes or until desired thickness.

Makes 1¼ cups (300 mL).

PINEAPPLE JAM

Combine in a saucepan until dissolved:

1 tbsp.	**(15 mL)**	**cornstarch**
2 tbsp.	**(30 mL)**	**unsweetened concentrated pineapple juice, defrosted**

Stir in:

⅔ cup	**(150 mL)**	**well-drained unsweetened crushed pineapple**
¾ cup	**(175 mL)**	**juice drained from crushed pineapple**
1 tbsp.	**(15 mL)**	**lemon juice**

Cook and stir until thick and clear.

Makes 1¼ cups (300 mL). See photograph page 80A.

PEACH JAM

Mix in a saucepan until starch dissolves:

½ tsp.	**(2 mL)**	**cornstarch**
6 tbsp.	**(90 mL)**	**unsweetened concentrated apple juice, defrosted**
2	**(2)**	**peaches, peeled, cored, crushed OR**
16	**(16)**	**slices canned peaches, drained, crushed**

Bring to a boil, then simmer and stir 2 minutes longer.

Add:

½ tsp.	**(2 mL)**	**almond extract**

Makes about 1 cup (250 mL).

VARIATION:

NECTARINE JAM: Replace 2 peaches with 2 nectarines, washed, cored and crushed.

ORANGE MARMALADE

Combine in a saucepan:

6 tbsp.	**(90 mL)**	**hot water**
1 tsp.	**(5 mL)**	**gelatine**

Add:

¼ tsp.	**(1 mL)**	**grated orange rind**
½	**(½)**	**orange, peeled, cut in fine pieces**
½ cup	**(125 mL)**	**unsweetened concentrated orange juice, defrosted**

Bring to a rolling boil. Remove from heat.

Makes 1 cup (250 mL)

Treats

COCONUT BALLS

Beat until smooth:

4.4 oz. (125 g) cream cheese, cubed, room temp.
1 tbsp. (15 mL) noninstant skim milk powder
4 tbsp. (60 mL) any jam, pages 96 to 99
½ tsp. (2 mL) vanilla
2 tsp. (10 mL) unsweetened concentrated fruit juice

Mix in:

½ cup (125 mL) toasted shredded coconut

Chill 1 hour for easier shaping. Form into small balls. Roll in toasted shredded coconut. Chill until ready to serve.

Makes 26.

VARIATION:

NUTTY BALLS: Replace vanilla with almond extract and toasted shredded coconut with roasted chopped nuts.

APRICOT BON BON

Steam 20 minutes over boiling water:

1 cup (250 mL) dried apricots
1 cup (250 mL) raisins

Put through fine knife of food chopper.

Add and stir until blended:

2 tbsp. (30 mL) unsweetened concentrated orange juice
1 tsp. (5 mL) vanilla
¼ tsp. (1 mL) grated orange rind

Mix in thoroughly:

2 tbsp. (30 mL) noninstant skim milk powder

Pick up 1 tsp. (5 mL) of the mixture. Shape into a ball. Roll in finely chopped nuts or toasted coconut.

Makes about 30.

ORANGE-LEMON DELIGHTS

Stand container in hot water until dissolved:

¾ cup	**(175 mL)**	**water**
3 tbsp.	**(45 mL)**	**gelatine**

Stir in:

3 tbsp.	**(45 mL)**	**lemon juice**
½ cup	**(125 mL)**	**unsweetened concentrated orange juice**
½ tsp.	**(2 mL)**	**grated orange rind**
¼ tsp.	**(1 mL)**	**grated lemon rind**

Chill until partially set. Beat on high until volume doubles. Pour into a small, shallow, buttered pan. Chill until firm. Cut into squares, triangles or any desired shapes. Coat with toasted shredded coconut. Serves 4.

NUT CRISP

Cook and stir over low heat until thick and smooth; cool:

3 tbsp.	**(45 mL)**	**unsweetened concentrated fruit juice**
6	**(6)**	**pitted dates, chopped**

Make fine crumbs, see page 8, with:

8	**(8)**	**soda crackers**

Place crumbs in bowl, add date mixture and:

5 tbsp.	**(75 mL)**	**chunky peanut butter**
2 tbsp.	**(30 mL)**	**finely chopped nuts**

Mix well. Shape into small balls. Roll in finely chopped nuts. Makes 12.

FRUIT PATTIES

Steam 20 minutes over boiling water:

1 cup	**(250 mL)**	**raisins**
1 cup	**(250 mL)**	**pitted dates**
9	**(9)**	**prunes, pitted**
4	**(4)**	**figs, stems removed**
10	**(10)**	**dried apricots**

Put fruit through food chopper using coarse blade. Mix thoroughly. Form into small balls. Flatten to ¼" (6 mm) to form patties. Coat with finely chopped nuts. Store in a covered jar or wrap individually. Makes 44.

Beverages

LEMONADE

Combine in a tall glass:

4 tsp.	**(20 mL)**	**lemon juice, chilled**
1 cup	**(250 mL)**	**ice water**
2 tbsp.	**(30 mL)**	**unsweetened concentrated pineapple OR apple juice, defrosted**

If preferred, add ice cubes. Garnish with a slice of lemon.

Serves 1.

VARIATION:

HOT LEMONADE: Make Lemonade recipe in a 10 oz. (284 mL) mug, but replace ice water with hot or boiling water.

PINK LEMONADE

Combine in a tall glass:

4 tsp.	**(20 mL)**	**lemon juice, chilled**
1 cup	**(250 mL)**	**ice water**
3 tbsp.	**(45 mL)**	**unsweetened red grape juice, chilled**
4 tsp.	**(20 mL)**	**unsweetened concentrated pineapple OR apple juice, defrosted**

If preferred, add ice cubes. Garnish with a slice of lemon.

Serves 1.

ICE CUBES FOR SPECIAL OCCASIONS:

Make decorative ice cubes by adding pitted cherries, pineapple cubes, carrot curls, olives or cocktail onions to the water in ice cube trays before freezing.

For colourful ice cubes, replace the water with tomato or fruit juices.

GRAPE SODA DRINK

Measure into a tall glass:

⅔ cup (150 mL) unsweetened grape juice, chilled

Stir in lightly:

½ cup (125 mL) soda water, chilled

If preferred, add ice cubes. Serve at once.

Serves 1.

ORANGE SODA DRINK

Measure into a tall glass:

3 tbsp. (45 mL) unsweetened concentrated orange juice, defrosted

Stir in lightly:

1 cup (250 mL) soda water, chilled

If preferred, add ice cubes. Serve at once.

Serves 1.

FRUIT PUNCH

Combine:

1 cup (250 mL) unsweetened pineapple juice
¾ cup (175 mL) unsweetened orange juice
6 tbsp. (90 mL) unsweetened concentrated apple juice, defrosted
2 cups (500 mL) soda water

Measure into each of 4 tall glasses:

¼ cup (50 mL) crushed ice

Pour juice mixture over crushed ice. Serve at once.

Serves 4.

HOT TODDY

Combine in a saucepan:

1¼ cups	**(300 mL)**	**unsweetened grape juice**
⅔ cup	**(150 mL)**	**unsweetened grapefruit juice**
⅓ cup	**(75 mL)**	**unsweetened orange juice**
1 tbsp.	**(15 mL)**	**lemon juice**
1	**(1)**	**cinnamon stick**

Heat to boiling; reduce to medium-low. Cover and simmer 10 minutes. Remove cinnamon stick.

Stir in:

2 tbsp.	**(30 mL)**	**brandy (optional)**

Serve immediately.

Makes 4 small servings.

HOT SPICED APPLE JUICE

Combine in a saucepan:

4 cups	**(1 L)**	**unsweetened apple juice**
2	**(2)**	**cinnamon sticks**
10	**(10)**	**whole cloves**
10	**(10)**	**allspice berries**

Heat to boiling; reduce to medium-low. Cover and simmer 10 minutes. Strain. Serve hot.

Serves 4.

EGGNOG

Beat until blended:

1	**(1)**	**fresh egg, beaten**
¼ tsp.	**(1 mL)**	**vanilla**
1 tbsp.	**(15 mL)**	**unsweetened concentrated apple juice, defrosted**
1 cup	**(250 mL)**	**cold milk**

Pour into a tall glass. Sprinkle lightly with nutmeg.

Serves 1.

FROTHY ORANGE MILK

Beat on high until frothy:

⅓ cup	**(75 mL)**	**instant skim milk powder OR**
2 tbsp.	**(30 mL)**	**noninstant skim milk powder**
1 cup	**(250 mL)**	**unsweetened orange juice, chilled**
¼ tsp.	**(1 mL)**	**vanilla**

Serve at once.

Serves 1.

PEACH MILK

Blend until smooth:

1	**(1)**	**peach, peeled, sliced**
1 cup	**(250 mL)**	**unsweetened apple OR pineapple juice, chilled**
⅓ cup	**(75 mL)**	**instant skim milk powder OR**
2 tbsp.	**(30 mL)**	**noninstant skim milk powder**

Serve at once.

Serves 1.

BANANA MILK

Blend until smooth:

1	**(1)**	**ripe banana, sliced**
1½ cups	**(375 mL)**	**cold milk**

Serve at once.

Serves 2.

VARIATION:

BANANA PINEAPPLE MILK: Add ¼ cup (50 mL) undrained, unsweetened, crushed pineapple before blending.

ORANGE MILK SHAKE

Place in a mixing cup or a tall container:

1 OR 2	**(1 OR 2)**	**scoops vanilla ice cream**
2 tbsp.	**(30 mL)**	**unsweetened concentrated orange juice**
1 cup	**(250 mL)**	**milk**

Whip until well blended. Serve in a tall glass with a long straw.

Serves 1.

ORANGE ICE CREAM SODA

Place in a tall glass:

1 OR 2	**(1 OR 2)**	**scoops vanilla ice cream**
3 tbsp.	**(45 mL)**	**unsweetened concentrated orange juice**

Slowly pour in while beating with a soda spoon until frothy:

¾ cup	**(175 mL)**	**soda water**

Serve at once with the soda spoon and a long straw.

Serves 1.

VARIATION:

PINEAPPLE ICE CREAM SODA: Replace orange juice with concentrated pineapple juice and add 2 tbsp. (30 mL) unsweetened crushed pineapple. Complete as for the Orange Ice Cream Soda.

YOGURT BANANA DRINK

Blend until smooth:

1	**(1)**	**banana, sliced**
1 cup	**(250 mL)**	**unsweetened fruit juice, chilled**
1 cup	**(250 mL)**	**plain yogurt**

Serve immediately.

Serves 2-3.

VARIATION:

YOGURT PEACH DRINK: Make Yogurt Banana Drink recipe but replace banana with 2 medium peaches, peeled and sliced.

INDEX

BEVERAGES

Eggnog.................................104
Hot Apple Juice, Spiced..............104
Hot Lemonade.........................102
Hot Toddy...............................104
Ice Cream Soda, Orange..............106
Ice Cream Soda, Pineapple...........106
Lemonade...............................102
Lemonade, Pink........................102
Milk
Banana Milk............................105
Banana Pineapple Milk...............105
Orange Milk, Frothy..................105
Peach Milk.............................105
Milk Shake, Orange...................106
Punch
Fruit Punch............................103
Soda Drinks
Grape Soda Drink.....................103
Orange Soda Drink...................103
Yogurt Banana Drink.................106
Yogurt Peach Drink...................106

BUTTERS, JAMS AND SPREADS

Butters
Apple Butter........................... 95
Garlic Butter or Margarine........... 94
Lemon Butter or Margarine........... 93
Orange Butter or Margarine.......... 93
Parsley Butter or Margarine......... 94
Peanut Butter.......................... 94
Whipped Butter or Margarine......... 93
Jams
Apricot Jam............................ 96
Date Jam............................... 97
Fig Jam................................. 97
Fruit Jam............................... 98
Nectarine Jam.......................... 99
Peach Jam.............................. 99
Pear Jam............................... 98
Pineapple Jam.......................... 98
Plum Jam, Fresh....................... 96
Prune Jam.............................. 97
Strawberry Jam I...................... 96
Strawberry Jam II..................... 96
Orange Marmalade..................... 99
Spreads
Cottage Cheese Spread............... 95
Cream Cheese Spread................. 95
Grape Jelly Spread.................... 94

CAKE AND CAKE DESSERTS

Apricot Cake, Dried.................. 23
Baked Alaska.......................... 29
Banana Cake........................... 21
Boston Cream Pie..................... 19
Carrot Cake............................ 24
Carrot Date Cake...................... 25
Coffee Cake, Crunchy Topping........ 26
Coffee Cake, Streusel Topping....... 26
Dutch Apple Cake..................... 25
Fruitcake, Dried Fruit................. 23
Fruit Cake, Fresh...................... 22
Fruit Flan.............................. 20
Fruit Flan, Custard.................... 21
Jelly Roll, Orange-Lemon............. 28
Layer Cake, Pineapple................ 28
Plain Cake.............................. 18
Sponge Cake........................... 19
Upside-Down Cake, Apple............ 27
Upside-Down Cake, Pineapple....... 27

COOKIES, BARS, SQUARES AND TURNOVERS

Bars
Fig Bars................................ 44
Jam Bars............................... 43
Pineapple Coconut Bars............... 43
Cookies
Apple Cookies, Spicy.................. 36
Apricot Jam Cookies.................. 38
Carob Cookies......................... 39
Coconut Cookies...................... 37
Coconut Macaroons................... 40
Cream Cheese Cookies............... 40
Date Cookies.......................... 38
Jam-Filled Oatmeal Cookies......... 42
Peanut Butter Cookies............... 37

Peanut Macaroons.................. 40
Wheat Germ Cookies............... 41

Squares

Date Squares...................... 44

Turnovers

Date Turnovers 41
Raisin Turnovers.................. 41

DESSERTS: BAKED, COLD & FRUIT

Baked Desserts

Apple Crisp 46
Cheesecake, Orange-Lemon 48
Cobbler, Blueberry................. 45
Cream Puffs........................ 47
Eclairs 47

Cold Desserts

Bavarian, Fruit 53
Bavarian, Low-Calorie Fruit.......... 52
Bavarian, Low-Calorie Lemon 53
Blanc Mange, Orange 55
Blanc Mange, Pineapple........... 55
Cheesecake, No-Bake Pineapple.... 54
Custard Blanc Mange, Orange 55
Custard Blanc Mange, Pineapple.... 55
Fruit in Jelly, Fresh 52
Ice Cream, Vanilla.................. 57
Jellied Pineapple 51
Jelly, Grape 50
Jelly, Lemon 50
Jelly, Orange 50
Jelly, Pineapple.................... 50
Jelly, Raspberry................... 51
Mousse, Strawberry................ 57
Quick Banana Dessert............. 54
Sherbet, Orange.................... 56
Snow, Apple 53
Whip, Jelly......................... 51
Whip, Yogurt Jelly 51
Yogurt 55
Yogurt, Frozen Banana 56
Yogurt, Frozen Pineapple 56
Yogurt, Fruit 56

Fruit Desserts

Applesauce......................... 46
Baked Apple........................ 46
Fruit Whip 49
Prune Whip 49
Stewed Figs 49
Stewed Prunes 48

FILLINGS

Apple.............................. 61
Cottage Cheese 59
Cream 58
Custard............................ 59
Custard Cream 59
Date............................... 60
Fig................................ 60
Orange............................. 58
Orange-Lemon...................... 58
Pineappple 60
Raisin 61

FROSTINGS AND TOPPINGS

Frostings

Carob Frosting 33
Cottage Cheese Frosting........... 33
Cream Cheese Frosting 33
Pineapple-Cheese Frosting......... 32
Seven-Minute Frosting 34

Icing, Buttery 34

Meringue........................ 34

Broiled Applesauce Meringue...... 35
Broiled Banana Meringue.......... 35
Orange Meringue.................. 35

Toppings

Apple-Cheese Topping............. 32
Low-Calorie Whipped Topping..... 31
Pineapple Topping 32
Whipped Orange Topping.......... 31

Whipped Cream 30

Low-Calorie Whipped Cream........ 31
Mock Whipped Cream 30

HELPFUL TIPS

Bread, freshen stale 92
Cakes, more even baking of 22
Coconut, toast..................... 61
Cookies, easy drop 36
Egg, differentiate cooked........... 75
Egg, dividing 35
Egg, shell easily.................... 74
Egg, test freshness of 17

Egg whites, beating 17
Egg whites, fold in 17
Fine crumbs 8
Fruit, keep fresh cut 22
Fruit, prevent sinking 22
Fruit juice, store concentrated 18
Gelatine desserts, unmould 68
Ice cubes for special occasions 102
Meringue, prevent from shrinking 17
Milk, make sour 71
Muffins, tender 83
Oven, keep clean 17
Oven temperature, accuracy of 5
Pies, best results in making 7
Popovers, prevent soggy 91
Puddings, steam 68
Skim milk powder 61

MUFFINS, POPOVERS, QUICK BREADS & SCONES

Muffins
Apple Muffins 84
Blueberry Muffins 84
Carrot Muffins 84
Cheese Muffins 84
Cornmeal Muffins 86
Date Muffins 85
Fig Oatmeal Muffins 86
Filled Muffins 84
100% Whole-Wheat Muffins 84
Pineapple Muffins 85
Plain Muffins 83
Raisin Bran Muffins 88
Sour Milk Muffins 84
Wheat-Germ Muffins 88
Popovers 91
Popovers, Oatmeal 92
Quick Breads
Banana Bran Bread 89
Cheese Bread 87
Date Bran Bread 89
Lemon Bread 87
Lemon-Walnut Bread 87
Wheat-Germ Bread 90
Zucchini Bread 90
Scones 92

PANCAKES AND CRÊPES

Apple Pancakes 69
Sliced Apple Pancakes 72
Banana Pancakes 69
Blini (Russian Pancakes) 74
Blueberry Pancakes 69
Bran Pancakes 70
Cornmeal Pancakes 71
Cottage Cheese Pancakes 70
Crêpes 72
Crêpe Cake, Apple-Cheese 73
Crêpes Suzette, Strawberry 75
Oatmeal Pancakes 71
Plain Pancakes 69
Sour Milk Pancakes 69
Whole-Wheat Pancakes 69

PIES AND TARTS

Pastries
Baked Pie Shell 7
Cheese Pastry 8
Crumb Pie Crust 8
One-Crust Pie Pastry 6
One-Crust Pie Pastry, using oil 7
Two-Crust Pie Pastry 5
Two-Crust Pie Pastry, using oil 6
Pies
Apple Pie 14
Banana Cream Pie 12
Blueberry Pie, Fresh 13
Coconut Cream Pie 12
Coconut Pie, Self-Crusting 9
Cranberry-Apple Pie 10
Cream Pie 12
Custard Pie 11
Lemon Chiffon Pie 10
Peach Pie, Fresh 13
Pineapple Sponge Pie 12
Pumpkin Pie 11
Raisin Pie 14
Strawberry Pie, Fresh 9
Tarts
Apple Meringue Tarts 17
Banana Cream Tarts 15
Fresh Fruit Tarts 16
Kiwi Cream Tarts 15
Lemon Tarts 16

Pineapple Tarts.................... 16
Tart Shells, Baked 15
Tart Shells, Unbaked.............. 15

PUDDINGS

Bread Pudding...................... 67
Raisin Bread Pudding.............. 67
Carrot Pudding....................... 64
Cornmeal Pudding 64
Fruit Grunt............................ 65
Rice Pudding 65
Sago Pudding 67
Self-Saucing Apple Pudding.......... 68
Self-Saucing Peach Pudding.......... 68
Soufflé, Orange-Lemon.............. 66
Steamed Puddings
Christmas Pudding.................. 62
Date and Walnut Pudding 63
Fruit and Walnut Pudding.......... 63
Tapioca Pudding, Old-Fashioned.... 67
Tapioca Pudding, Orange........... 66

SWEET SAUCES AND SYRUPS

Sweet Sauces
Apricot Sauce....................... 76
Blueberry Sauce 77
Brandy Sauce....................... 79
Cottage Cheese Dressing........... 80
Custard Sauce 76
Foamy Sauce 77
Fruit Sauce.......................... 78
Fruit-Juice Sauce 78
Lemon Sauce 78
Orange Sauce 78
Orange Sauce, Chunky.............. 78
Orange-Lemon Sauce 78
Orange-Raisin Sauce 78
Raspberry Sauce.................... 80
Rum Sauce........................... 79
Strawberry Sauce 80
Syrups
Apple Syrup, using apple juice...... 82
Apple Syrup, using applesauce 82
Fig Syrup 81
Pineapple Syrup 81
Raisin Syrup 81

TREATS

Apricot Bon Bon 100
Coconut Balls.........................100
Fruit Patties 101
Nut Crisp 101
Nutty Balls............................100
Orange-Lemon Delights.............100

SHARE **THE SUGARLESS COOKBOOK** WITH A FRIEND

Please send ____________ copies of **THE SUGARLESS COOKBOOK** at **$10.95** per book, plus **$1.50** (total order) for postage and handling:

Number of books __________ x $10.95 = $______

Handling charge ______________________ + $1.50

Total enclosed ________________________ ______

NAME: ____

STREET: ______________________________________

CITY: ____________________ **PROV./STATE** ____________

COUNTRY ____________________ **POSTAL CODE/ZIP** ____________

Please make cheque or money order payable to:

HUM Publishing
395 Second Avenue
Ottawa, Ontario
K1S 2J3

Price subject to change/U.S. and International orders payable in U.S. funds

For fund raising or volume purchases, contact Hum Publishing for volume rates

- -

SHARE **THE SUGARLESS COOKBOOK** WITH A FRIEND

Please send ____________ copies of **THE SUGARLESS COOKBOOK** at **$10.95** per book, plus **$1.50** (total order) for postage and handling:

Number of books __________ x $10.95 = $______

Handling charge ______________________ + $1.50

Total enclosed ________________________ ______

NAME: ____

STREET: ______________________________________

CITY: ____________________ **PROV./STATE** ____________

COUNTRY ____________________ **POSTAL CODE/ZIP** ____________

Please make cheque or money order payable to:

HUM Publishing
395 Second Avenue
Ottawa, Ontario
K1S 2J3

Price subject to change/U.S. and International orders payable in U.S. funds

For fund raising or volume purchases, contact Hum Publishing for volume rates